THE BIG Q

*

COLLEGE OF HIGHER EDUCATION

200

R. E. UNIT

THE BIG QUESTIONS

Believing with Heart and Mind

ROD GARNER

*

First published in Great Britain 1995
Society for Promoting Christian Knowledge
Holy Trinity Church
Marylebone Road
London NW1 4DU

© Rod Garner 1995

All rights reserved. No part of this book may be reproduced or
transmitted in any form or by any means, electronic or mechanical,
including photocopying, recording, or by any information storage and
retrieval system, without permission in writing from the publisher.

British Library Cataloguing-in-Publication Data
A catalogue record for this book is available from the British Library

ISBN 0-281-04797-9

Typeset by Dorwyn Ltd, Rowlands Castle, Hants
Printed in Great Britain by
BPC Paperbacks Ltd

For Christine:
companion, lover, friend.
With love and gratitude.

ACKNOWLEDGEMENTS

---

*

All Desires Known by Janet Morley, © SPCK 1992. Used by permission of the author.

One Man's Prayers by George Appleton, © SPCK 1967. Used by permission of the publisher.

Contemporary Prayers for Public Worship edited by Caryl Micklem, © SCM Press 1967. Used by permission of the publisher.

'An African Creed' in *Christianity Rediscovered* by Vincent J. Donovan, © SCM Press, 1982. Used by permission of the publisher.

Enfolded in Love by Julian of Norwich, © Darton, Longman & Todd 1980. Used by permission of the publisher.

Love's Endeavour, Love's Expense by W.H. Vanstone, © Darton, Longman & Todd 1977. Used by permission of the publisher.

'A Fifteenth-Century Irish Poet Tadhg Óg Ó hUiggin' in *A Celtic Miscellany* by Kenneth Hurlstone Jackson, © Routledge and Kegan Paul. Used by permission of the publisher.

'Dust' in *The Collected Poems of Elizabeth Jennings* by Elizabeth Jennings, © Carcanet 1987. Used by permission of the publisher.

Scriptural quotations from the *New English Bible*, © Oxford University Press and Cambridge University Press 1961, 1970.

Extracts from *The Book of Common Prayer*, the rights in which are vested in the Crown, are reproduced by permission of the Crown's Patentee, Cambridge University Press.

'Not Waving But Drowning' in *The Collected Poems of Stevie Smith*, edited by James MacGibbon, © Penguin 20th Century Classics. Used by permission.

Excerpt from the poems of William Blake, quoted by J. Bronowski in *William Blake and the Age of Revolution*, © Routledge and Kegan Paul, 1972. Used by permission of the publisher.

Extracts from the Authorized Version of the Bible (The King James Bible), the rights in which are vested in the Crown, are reproduced by permission of the Crown's Patentee, Cambridge University Press.

CONTENTS

*

FOREWORD

*

This book is about living *with* God in *this* world. It will not be of any great interest to people whose personal relationship with God monopolizes their attention, and concentrates their concern on their individual destiny *beyond* this world. Nor, at the other extreme, will it much interest those who, for intellectual or emotional reasons, are committed to the propositions that God does not exist, and that beyond this world there is *nothing*.

But most of us live at some point in the spectrum between these extremes. Nearest to the first extreme are those who aspire to live with God, but find this world an increasingly unsatisfactory place in which to do so: nearest to the second are those who aspire to getting the best out of this world but, though accepting the possibility that God exists, find his existence irrelevant to their aspiration.

It is to and for people who live somewhere within this spectrum that Mr Garner has written his book. He is a parish priest of the Church of England who in his twenties made the move from personnel management in the world of business to the study of theology in preparation for ordination. His earlier career has left its mark on his present ministry. It has made him notably efficient in the management of his time and work in parishes where there is much to be done and, more than that, it has given him experience of, and insight into, the possibility and process of reconciliation between people who have different interests and opposite points of view. He is well aware that reconciliation neither achieves nor aims at decisive victory by one side and abject surrender by the other: that it proceeds by small steps rather than giant strides: and that either or both sides to a dispute may be motivated not only by the facts which they present but also by hidden agendae, consisting not of facts but of feelings, which will block negotiations, unless and until, they are brought into the open.

Mr Garner writes in the tone of a reconciler, a mediator. He himself believes that it is possible to live with God in this world—or, more exactly, to draw gradually nearer to doing so. But he recognizes, and emphasizes that serious difficulties stand in the way—difficulties both intellectual and existential. He recognizes on the one hand, for instance, the intellectual difficulty of squaring the existence of a good God with the fact that the world is riddled with appalling suffering, which is neither man-made nor deserved. He recognizes on the other hand the existential difficulty of accepting that the love and beauty which we experience in the world, and the senses of obligation and shame which we feel, consist in reality of nothing more than the movement and interaction of material particles in our brains and bodies.

Over such great matters Mr Garner writes thoughtfully and perceptively. He neither resolves the difficulty nor claims to do so, but he makes contributions to the debate which are neither platitudes nor trivialities. He never papers over difficulties by complacent references either to 'what our faith teaches' or to 'what science proves'. The last thing he wants is that we should suppress our awareness of such difficulties, or pretend that they do not exist: for if we do we shall cease to 'use our brains' about them, and they will become 'unmentionables' which, if mentioned in company, make us acutely embarrassed. Mr Garner is convinced that the brains of 'ordinary people' are quite capable of 'thinking their way' into and even through the core of deep problems, and that this capacity is enhanced in discussion with others which is free from embarrassment, and in which hidden agendae are brought to light.

So this book is a very valuable contribution to such discussion among people who stand at different points within that 'spectrum' of opinion and life style to which I have referred. As

I have said, Mr Garner does not claim that he has resolved all or any of the problems which are likely to arise in such discussion or 'found a formula' to which all the participants can agree. On the contrary, he himself writes in his introduction that his concern has been to get 'not from A to Z but from A to C interestingly' in the hope that others will continue the exploration.

He certainly writes *interestingly*. His reading is wide and his quotations are plucked from a great range of sources—from Jewish Rabbis to Voltaire, from Freud to St Augustine, from Kruschev to Sam Goldwyn. Because he lives 'in this world' he has a sense of humour and moving stories to tell from his own experience; and from his own pen come some memorable phrases—not least his reference to Dr Johnson as 'that wise and vulnerable Christian gentleman'. It is to be noted that at the end of each chapter we are offered, as a kind of bonus, a number of passages 'for reflection'—many of them unfamiliar to most of us. These too are chosen from a wide variety of sources, and not one is unworthy to be chosen.

Mr Garner's responsibilities extend at present beyond his parish in Hull. He is also Lay Training Officer throughout the Archdeaconry of the East Riding. As such his role is to promote and organize courses of study through which people from different churches and towns may come to a fuller and more articulate understanding of the Christian faith that they share. I think that it will be Revd Garner's hope and purpose that these courses shall not only be a direct benefit to the people who take part in them, but also be an indirect benefit to those many others with whom they associate in their homelife and work and leisure. For many of those others will no doubt be living at that point in the spectrum of belief at which God appears not so much 'non-existent' as 'irrelevant'; and it must surely be a benefit to them if those professing Christians with whom they associate can sometimes talk with them about the things of God without embarrassment, naturally, frankly, thoughtfully, wrestling with problems rather than prescribing solutions, laying open their ignorance as well as their insights and their hesitations as well as their certainties. It is in this tone that Mr Garner addresses his readers in this admirable book. It is to be hoped that, having taken us so interestingly 'from A to C' he will in the future take us on to E and G . . . and who knows how far?

W. H. Vanstone

*I want to understand something of the truth
which my heart believes and loves.*

(St Anselm, *c.* 1033–1109, Archbishop of Canterbury,
Teacher of the Faith)

INTRODUCTION

*

NOT FAR FROM my hand as I write this introduction lies a bookmark inscribed with some words of Martin Luther: 'One does not become a theologian simply by reading and studying but rather through conflict, temptation, being condemned, dying and living.' These words made their mark on me when I first read them shortly before being ordained to the Anglican ministry in 1978. Sixteen years of hard and varied experience in urban parishes combined, increasingly, with the work of theological education have convinced me that Luther was right. At one level theology requires us to use our heads—to hold on to our brains as best we can, so that faith does not succumb to the twin perils of fundamentalism or plain nonsense. And in a confused and confusing world where many are sceptical or scornful about religious claims, clarity is called for concerning what we profess to believe and how it relates to the rest of our lives.

This is not to say that theology is nothing more than an intellectual pursuit for the high-minded—for scholars and those who relish the cut and thrust of conference debate. Faith can never be a purely rational affair because people do not suffer or die for the sake of a tidy conclusion. What theology has to do is unite heart and mind in a way that does justice to our intuitions and imagination as well as our ideas, and make sense of the muddle of our lives. Theological truth has to be felt and appropriated in the daily struggle to be human and faithful—often in the most unpromising situations. It matters then that faith springs from firm foundations, resting more on truth and integrity than on the questionable need for certainty in an uncertain world.

1

INTRODUCTION

Apart from getting my own thoughts and reflections down on paper in some coherent form, my hope is that the following chapters will help and encourage anyone who is seeking to be a little more serious about faith: those whose hearts and minds require more nourishment than the meagre gruel much contemporary preaching seems able to provide; those who need to ask difficult questions—who want to explore what it means to believe in God without feeling threatened or embarrassed in the process; and those who lack the time to read large theological tomes, but want something more than pap.

The themes I've chosen could hardly be more weighty—too big in fact, some might think, to be included in so short a compass. The reader must be the judge. I hope that I shall not be found guilty, thereby incurring the verdict attributed to Sam Goldwyn—'on the surface profound, but deep down superficial'. In my defence, I ought to say that each chapter is meant to be neither definitive nor exhaustive in its scope. My concern throughout is not to get from A to Z but from A to C, interestingly, in the hope that others will complete the assignment as part of their own continuing exploration. The increasing round of courses, conferences, and quiet days that have made my work so satisfying in recent years lead me to believe that people are ready to take up the task with enthusiasm.

Given the aim of this book I cannot finish without expressing personal gratitude to those who have nurtured my own faith and understanding; in particular, to the late Father Frederick Osborn who set me on the road, and taught me about the beauty of holiness; and to Canon Bill Vanstone and Canon John Gain for their unfailing hospitality and breadth of vision.

Finally, my thanks to my wife Christine who typed the manuscript, and was gentle with her criticisms and warm in her support. And to my sons, Daniel and George, who suffered occasional silences dutifully, so their father could think; and demanded only trips to the cinema by way of modest recompense.

ONE

*

The Question of God

SOME YEARS AGO, a priest working in a run-down parish was asked why he was doing it—why the persistent hard slog for such pitiful returns? He replied, 'So that the rumour of God may not disappear completely'.[1] His remark will strike some as a little odd: after all, more people still go to church than watch football; cathedrals and churches are everywhere to be seen; bishops sit in the House of Lords and most British people regard themselves (if only nominally) as Christian. Enough evidence here, we might suppose, for the view that God is actually rather more than a rumour in our ambiguous world. Amidst 'change and decay' God remains an abiding and significant part of our landscape and language.

It's a comforting view, but one that fails to give a complete picture of what is actually going on. Many imposing church buildings have few worshippers in them; tourists rather than the faithful monopolize our cathedrals; children have difficulty reciting the Lord's Prayer and, repeatedly, we find ignorance of or indifference towards basic Christian truths. Returning to England after twenty-seven years as a bishop in the Church of South India, Lesslie Newbigin noted the 'cold contempt for the gospel' as he made fitful contact with ordinary people on the doorsteps of Birmingham.[2]

We have a curious situation then—one in which religious institutions and their leaders are still clearly visible, yet the truths to which they testify leave many lives untouched. Alongside what we might call the persistence of faith

3

manifested in the worship and witness of church congregations, there is a religious vacuum described by Rabbi Jonathan Sacks in his recent Reith Lectures as 'a God-shaped hole in our ozone layer'.[3] As late as the nineteenth century, people invoked God in various contexts: society, morality, politics, economics—in all these areas reference to God was still declared admissible (even though in some cases grudgingly). Now it seems that the notion of God languishes on the margin of our lives, lacking any currency at all except when we want or need to be religious.

On this view religion becomes a purely private matter, and God can be safely removed from the public world (where real life takes place) without it making any difference at all. Religion and society are separate entities: edit God out of the language, and our social world is still intact.

The tidiness of this theory should not blind us to the awareness that it is simply not supported by the facts. When, as in our own time, God is regarded as a bystander or a refugee from a former world of myth and superstition, what we actually see is not a society at ease with itself but one in which fragmentation, disorder, and the loss of shared values are all painfully evident.

To say this is not to engage in a tedious diatribe against a decadent society that has lost its bearings because it no longer recognizes God. The more important point is this: there can be little real hope of genuine human flourishing or community life when all we have to offer one another is a philosophy that amounts to 'each person doing that which is right in his own eyes'[4] without too much concern for others. Frank Sinatra singing 'I did it my way' is an anthem for a doomed age.

There has to be a better song—one that stresses meanings beyond self-assertiveness that are bound up with themes of kinship, human dignity, and responsibility. All of these we should note are biblically inspired, and flow naturally from the notion of the covenant between God and humanity.[5] Society is an extended family in which others—particularly the poor and the powerless—have a claim upon us. They are 'flesh of our flesh, bone of our bone'.[6] They are children of the same God.

There are good reasons, then, for us to tackle the question of God with a new urgency. What makes a society is not simply the latest piece of legislation from Westminster, but the shared traditions and insights that direct the way we should behave and govern our lives. Without these common values things fall apart with disarming ease, and 'community' becomes a weasel word meaning little more than the factional interests of any one particular grouping within society. By contrast, if we are able to acknowledge God in the structures of our common life, and see morality as the divine imperative that binds us together, we shall be able to think of society as the place where virtue is pursued and wrongdoing reproved. Voltaire, that eighteenth-century scourge of religious cant and dogma, was not being entirely cynical when he said: 'I want my lawyer, tailor, valets, even my wife to believe in God. I think that if they do, I shall be robbed less and cheated less.'[7]

Another powerful inducement to put God at the top of our agenda has to do with the integrity of what we profess to believe. Well before John Robinson wrote *Honest to God*,[8] too many intelligent people had come to regard the Christian story as improbable or untrue. They were more than ready to be serious about deep questions, but found traditional religious answers implausible. More than a generation on, has anything changed? The religious broadcaster Gerald Priestland running a series of programmes[9] on Radio 4 a decade ago was amazed to receive thousands of letters from listeners fascinated by the issues he raised, yet who apparently lacked any real contact with their local churches. They wanted to believe but couldn't—at least not on the basis of what they gleaned from the clergy.

Here we stand justly accused. Tired though we have been at times as a Church in our proclamation of God, we have not been slow to discourage deep thought and intellectual integrity. By a steady process of osmosis rather than outright dictum, we have encouraged our congregations not to think. Simple faith is declared to be a laudable aim, despite the fact that it entails a way of thinking about the world which, quite often, those outside the Church find unsatisfactory. And it will not do by way of cheap rejoinder to say 'so much the worse for them'.

Without conceding that the world sets our agenda, we are required to take its questions with genuine seriousness. The Kingdom of God, we should remember, is not to be confused with or restricted to the boundaries of the Church. Neither the biblical doctrine of creation, nor for that matter the teaching of Jesus, gives us any grounds for supposing that the Church figures more prominently in the divine purpose than the world which God loved so much 'that he gave his only Son so that everyone who believes in him may not perish but may have eternal life'.[10]

To recap: the health of the nation and the probity of our teaching should encourage us to find ways of setting forth our understanding of God that enable obstacles to belief to be addressed and overcome. By producing 'a better song', we might just invigorate our own faith, and enliven the deadened consciousness of modern society that renders the use of the term 'God' so very problematic.

But let us be honest and recognize at the outset that even as believers we have to face the question of what is the nature of the reality we are trying to describe when our thoughts turn to God? The gracious power and presence of the One who meets us, dwells in us, and yet transcends us has been testified to from the beginning by Christian faith.[11] If, as we believe, God is more than just the sum of our hopes, and possesses a reality beyond our minds and aspirations, where are we to find the concepts that will do justice to 'this most tremendous tale of all'?[12]

We have the Bible of course with its profusion of metaphors, images, and stories about God. But note how often they point to sheer mystery rather than definitive statement. God appears to Moses in the burning bush and reveals his name as I AM WHO I AM.[13] The encounter at one level is decisive: Moses stands on holy ground, and knows himself to be in the divine presence. Yet God does not throw himself at the prophet 'like a stone'. Beyond the disclosure, what God essentially *is* still remains hidden, elusive, incomplete—as if to remind us that even revelation is provisional. Put another way: the God who reveals himself to Moses is greater than what is revealed about God.

Part of us no doubt wants things to be a little more clear-cut than this, particularly if we are more at ease with plain truths than awesome mystery. In our concern to 'tell it straight' however, we can easily part company with Scripture: with St Paul who knew 'how unsearchable are the judgements of God and his ways past tracing out';[14] and with Jesus who makes hardly any direct statements about God, even God as Father. The latter theme never surfaces in his general teaching to the multitudes but only in intimate talk with disciples—or in prayer.

If all this still strikes us as special pleading—as the needless complication of what is essentially a simple gospel, we might ask ourselves a disarming question: '*What* do I love when I love God?' St Augustine poses this question to himself in his *Confessions*. In the chapters of the tenth book he struggles to provide an answer, but when all the analogies and metaphors at his disposal have been set aside he can only describe the object of his love in terms of poetic adoration:

> Thou didst call louder and louder and
> didst break through my deafness.
> Thou didst shine radiantly and more
> radiantly and didst penetrate my
> blindness.
> Thou didst blow and I came to breath
> and life, and breathe in thee.
> I did taste Thee, and I hunger and thirst after Thee.

Here we have the unmistakable language of deep Christian devotion which arises out of that profound sense of God to which saints and mystics alike have borne witness. What is striking is that the passage is authoritative without being authoritarian; it compels without cajoling us into a narrow way of thinking about God; it alerts us to the One who is unmistakably real yet in the end indubitably elusive. In this Decade of Evangelism, Augustine would surely caution us against reducing the gospel of God to little more than shallow slogans and 'sound-bites'. Something more subtle is called for if the religious dimension of life is to speak to an age which, as we have already noted, often finds the language of Christianity not only dead but indecipherable.

Courtesy and tact should shape our dealings with others as we seek to speak of the things of God. The Epistle to the Colossians says: 'Behave wisely towards those outside your own number . . . study how best to talk with each person you meet.' (Col. 4. 5–6) We cannot bludgeon people into belief, but we can surely try to awaken them to a deeper awareness of a reality beyond 'getting and spending', and to a possible meaning that illuminates the question which all those with lives to live and deaths to die cannot finally evade: 'What is it all for?'

The question touches more than the purpose of our particular lives; it should point us to the extraordinary fact that all about us lies a world inviting some sort of explanation. On a clear night we can look up and feel the awesome power and beauty of the universe—the countless stars each representing millions we cannot see. Beyond the Milky Way there is the teeming darkness, a 'world without end Amen'—everything known and unknown other than the grain of sand we live on. All this has been unfolding over billions of years: our distant origins as self-conscious beings stretch beyond Eden to the nuclear furnaces of burning stars, and our exquisite world with all its living forms is indebted to the vast pervasive order arising from the interrelation of matter, energy, space, and time.

We can only mouth banalities before this vision. Our speech loses its force and our mind is numbed by the immensity of that which it is challenged to comprehend. Before our thoughts even turn to God should we not be dazzled by the fact that there is a world at all? Instead of atoms and gravity and galaxies and stars; in place of the living cells that made humanity a possibility there could have been endless nothingness. The sheer improbability of the cosmos evolving in the way it has—so finely tuned, so constant in its governing laws—should induce in us a sense of wonder. Our amazement will have less to do with how the world is—its complexity and organization—than *that* it is—that against hugely improbable odds there is a planet Earth with persons on it seeking explanations for their comings and goings and the ache which lies at the heart of things.

Ultimately, it may prove to be the case that there is no explanation, and that the existence of an orderly world is compatible with the non-existence of a creator or designer. Evolutionary biology (or at least some of its practitioners[15]) seems content to explain all apparently purposeful forms of life as the outcome of unconscious and automatic processes with no end or purpose in view. How such a 'blind' evolutionary process has made possible the fact of mind—our proven ability to reflect on the system that has produced us, to evaluate it and transcend it—admits of no satisfactory answer. To explain mind (and the authority reason exerts over it) by saying that Nature has produced it as the oyster produces the pearl, is to explain 'six' by saying that it is 'half a dozen'—which is no explanation at all.

The fact that we observe such a high level of order in the world makes the appeal to chance as the organizing principle behind the creation seem less and less plausible. We could suppose that the plays attributed to Shakespeare came into being as a result of random typing by monkeys. But it is not a proposition that any reflective person would rush to defend. A more cogent explanation—and one we should note that is deeply embedded in human consciousness—is that the existence of a complex yet structured world leads us to the notion of a supreme cause or being. Creation presupposes a creator.

This is no novel thought. The prophet Jeremiah lived more than two thousand years ago at a time when the existence of a creator-god of some sort was taken for granted. What was in question was the extent of his knowledge, goodness, and power. Jeremiah argued from the harmony of the world that he was above all a reliable God. The regular behaviour of the creation demonstrated the reliability of the Creator who established the 'covenant of the day and night' and 'the ordinances of heaven and earth'.[16] But having established a creation God did not then leave the world to its own devices. The New Testament develops Jeremiah's insight, and reminds us that the doctrine of creation is not just about the beginning of the universe at a point in time. It embraces the more profound truth that God continues to sustain it and us. He is the One in whom 'we live and have our being'.[17] On closer inspection we can see that the Christian doctrine of creation is also one of continuous preservation.

More than rational assent is required here to grasp the full significance of what is being said. Confronted by something in the world we can ask how it comes to be there—meaning not just 'What got it started?' but 'What keeps it going?' It cannot be that the thing in question causes itself to exist for that would be to suppose that it pre-existed itself which is impossible. All we should finish up with on this view is a never-ending series of things caused to be and causing to be. If we set this notion aside we are left with the more intelligible idea that all things—the basic constituents of nature, even time itself—owe their continued existence to God as sustainer and preserver. This is in keeping with the Old Testament concept of a 'living God' dynamic in action, and a cosmos permanently in need of its Creator's supporting will.[18]

Surely our imagination cannot need more than this—the sudden realization that the whole enterprise of life—the continuity of the stars, the Earth's rocks, the manifold grass and waters, and our own uncertain existence is held in being by God. In a way that was perhaps not entirely clear before, we see that all is gift—'it is he who has made us and not we ourselves.'[19] And this can lead us to adoration. For our sense of dependence, far from being oppressive or demeaning, is, to our joy and delight, the means of our flourishing and our peace.

In one sense nothing extravagant is being claimed here. Our belief in God does not depend upon privileged access or specialized knowledge denied to other people. We start by knowing the world in which we live, and reason to God's existence from that. There is, in other words, raw data—what we and others perceive by means of our senses—which gives substance to our beliefs. There is a world and there is clear evidence of design.

There is also our awareness of moral obligation—the insistent voice of conscience that compels us to act in a particular way and rebukes us if we fail. A child falls into the water and our duty is to plunge in to the rescue. The drowning child is not a bare fact but a compelling one—she has a family and a future and must be saved. She is a person, not a parcel. That we set our own fears and safety aside, and involve ourselves in her plight (rather than contemplate her from a safe distance) is a deeply significant fact—the more so once we realize just how much of our time and energy are normally devoted to self-interest.

An observable feature of the world and human relationships is our distinctive sense of 'oughtness'—as the Book of Common Prayer puts it: 'We have left undone those things which we ought to have done; and we have done those things which we ought not to have done.'[20] Not only do we recognize the moral claims that situations and people make upon us (claims which frequently go well beyond duty or any notion of fairness); we are also painfully aware on occasions of our inability or refusal to meet them.

Given the choice between rescuing a priceless Rembrandt or a pregnant woman from a fire, we know, morally speaking, what our duty is. In the same way, we sense intuitively that wickedness, lies, and treachery are foul deeds and that mercy, truth, and honour have abiding worth. Right and wrong, in other words, are not just useful human conventions; the 'oughtness' that leads us to embrace one and reject the other is an ineradicable 'habit of the heart'—part of what we might call our moral ecology, and a world removed from mere sentiment or emotion.

Something more than prudence or, for that matter, piety drives us to sacrifice everything for the sake of a principle or a person, and it does seem that we can no more evade our sense of obligation than we can escape from our shadow. Believers and non-believers stand on common ground here—both alike can recognize moral claims as facts. But we should wish to make a further step and say that in order to make sense of morality—to give some cogency to our moral endeavours—we actually need a focus. The things we give a damn about, and may even be prepared to die for, find their final justification and value in the love of God whose mercy extends over all things. There is something satisfying to emotion and intellect in the awareness that principles, personal relationships, and moral passion are grounded in the love of God, and in so doing reflect the nature of One who is wholly good and in whose image we are made.[21]

None of this should lead us to say that the good deeds of unbelievers lack worth. Often they will do what is more than could reasonably be required of them and sometimes at great personal cost. But without God, their actions, though valid in themselves, seem to constitute a morality that lacks final integration.

We are back, indirectly, to the 'What's it all for?' question. The things which engage us most deeply are in the end disconnected, unrelated, miscellaneous even, without a focus. We can, of course, make humanity our religion, and see the needs of others as the only necessary justification for our doing good. But humanity is not God, is not without blemish, has its dark side, and, and, of itself therefore, has no final claim on us—moral or otherwise. Only by recognizing the image of God in neighbour and stranger—the loving God who is the source and focus of our own moral life—can we begin to see that morality is in the end worthwhile because ultimately it makes sense. In seeking the good of others we are manifesting a kind of blueprint in the divine mind—a pale reflection of the goodness exemplified by God.

It should be obvious that nothing we have said so far amounts to proofs for God's existence. This is not our concern for even if a proof that could not be doubted suddenly emerged, would this not prove an obituary notice for faith? Faith would be superfluous and the question of God irrelevant because we had found the object of our quest. This prospect we can confidently say is hardly in view. Even our most ingenious and subtle arguments must fail to confine or locate God as an object or item in the field of human knowledge. For as the source and sustainer of all that is, it must be obvious that God is not and cannot be an object, entity, or person in the sense that we normally understand these terms. And to suppose that he could be understood in any of these ways is to run the risk of turning God into an idol of our own devising.

It is worth recalling at this point what lies behind the second commandment given at Sinai: 'You shall not make yourself a carved image or any likeness of anything in heaven or on earth beneath or in the waters under the earth; you shall not bow down to them or serve them.' (Exod. 20.4) Ancient peoples thought that wherever they established an image of their god, they could compel him to manifest himself there—conjure him up so to speak like the genie in the bottle. But Israel's God was not to be controlled in this way. He was sovereign, free, and beyond manipulation. It was God and not the people of Israel who had brought their sacred relationship into being, and who retained control of how it should be enjoyed. Uniquely then, among contemporary cultures, Israel was to have no means of summoning up her God. All her official

13

shrines remained imageless, and in archaeological excavations to date no image of a human male figure has been discovered.

If we take this wisdom to heart and remind ourselves that religion does not produce God as an object to be observed, there is nothing improper in our continuing to speak of God in personal terms—or, to express it more accurately—to think of him as 'not less than personal'. For a very good reason we can do no other: as believers (or aspiring believers) today, we have inherited the immensely long and rich experience of all those who have affirmed in their living and dying that there is One who makes a demand upon us, which is infinitely closer to the claim of a person than that of an impersonal object. God is someone to whom we can respond in worship, prayer, and adoration and, as we saw earlier, depend upon as our deepest and most abiding resource. The philosopher Martin Buber speaks for Jews and Christians alike when he writes:

> The description of God as a person is indispensable for everyone who like myself means by 'God' not a principle, not an idea . . . but him who enters into a direct relation with us in creative, revealing and redeeming acts, and thus makes it possible for us to enter into a direct relation with him. The ground and meaning of our existence constitutes a mutuality . . . such as can subsist only between persons.[22]

Something else needs to be said about the kind of truth being expressed here—about, in effect, the case we are making for God's existence. Christianity views truth not simply as something impersonal to be bandied about in propositions, but as a reality that is inwardly appropriated, and engages us at the deepest level of our existence. Truth on this view has always a personal dimension that is in turn corroborated by the community of truthfulness to which we belong.

Christian truth therefore is more than propositional: it is communal in the sense that it is vindicated by the shared experience of women and men who have constituted the Church down the centuries. And it is relational because it concerns the proper relationship of humanity, creation, and God. In short, we want to say that the search for God is not the vain pursuit of an illusion, and is more than a rationally defensible quest. It is part of a more comprehensive and interlocking system of beliefs that requires from us not only rationality but the readiness to embrace a particular way of life. As the ARCIC Final Report expresses it:

> The role of the Church as a community of faith and truthfulness under the guidance of the Holy Spirit is to sustain and unfold the transmission of revealed truth. This requires not only intellectual assent but also the response of the whole person.[23]

The 'revealed truth' to which the Report refers is for Christian faith grounded supremely in the person of Christ—the one in whom the Creator made himself accessible to his world. We have in Christ a new and developing appreciation of the kind of God we worship. While reason can go some way to arguing that there is a mind behind the universe, the death and resurrection of Jesus permit us to say that there is a heart as well. Accepting as we must that all our thoughts about God are to some extent conjectures, we have nevertheless in the resurrection of Jesus not the resuscitation of a corpse but the gift, to a man who had died a cruel death, of a new and indestructible life. And this was God's work—the initiative of the One who designated Jesus as Son of God 'by his resurrection from the dead'.[24]

That 'something happened' on that first Easter morning is hardly open to question once we acknowledge the transformation of a broken band of followers into the apostles and evangelists who were to 'turn the world upside down'. Even this, however, hardly constitutes a proof in the normal sense; something more than understanding is called for here if any real sense is to be made of Jesus' claim to be 'the way, the truth and the life'.[25] The conviction of the New Testament that in Jesus we see in human form the love which brought all creation into being and moves the sun and the other stars is compelling only when we progress beyond mere assent and are prepared to follow in the way. Only by responding to the words 'follow thou me' can we begin to grasp the ineffable mystery of the 'strange man on the cross,' and discover for ourselves what history and faith have claimed him to be—the agent of God's truth.

In this opening chapter we have advanced certain claims: that the existence of a good Earth in a cosmos of awesome symmetry turns our minds to the question of God; and that furthermore the moral law within us—the 'oughtness' that shapes our inner lives—reflects something of the nature of God himself. What this nature essentially is remains unfathomable, but our knowledge of Jesus and our experience of wonder suggest that our trust and hope are not confounded when they rest in God.

More could be said of our theme, and the next chapter will in fact say something about the reality of God as we encounter it in prayer. But before we turn the page a word about the temptation (desire, even) to give an explanation to everything.

The fact is that some questions—and the question of God is one of them—have no final solutions. What they reveal to us is the limits of our understanding. Instead of seeing this as some sort of deficiency it is better by far that we embrace this as part of our humanity. Then perhaps we can reach out to others with their questions and uncertainties, and show them that we all stand together under God. Let the book of Ecclesiasticus have the final word: 'However much we say, our words will always fall short; the end of the matter is: God is all.' (Ecclus. 43.27)

FOR REFLECTION

Lord God, we come to adore you. You are the ground of all
    that is.
You hold us in being, and without you we could not be.
Before we were born, before time began, before the uni-
    verse came into being, you were.
When time is finished, when the universe is no more, you
    will still be.
Nothing can take your power from you.
And in your presence we can only be silent before the mys-
    tery of your being, for no words of ours can do justice
    to your grandeur.

(A silence)

Yet you have spoken to us. Out of universal silence your
    living word has sprung..
You have spoken, and given form and beauty to the world.
You have spoken, and given purpose to human life.
You have spoken, and declared the forgiveness of our sin.
You have spoken, and freed us from the fear of death.

Lord Jesus Christ, divine Word, speak to us now.
Show us the beauty of life; unite us to the eternal purpose;
    remove our guilt; conquer the fear of death in our
    hearts.
Speak and let us hear, for your name's sake.

From Enfolded in Love *by* Julian of Norwich

See I Am God.
God is the still point at the centre.
There is no doer but he.

All this he showed me with great joy, saying, 'See, I am God. See I am in all things. See I do all things. See I never take my hands off my work, nor ever shall through all eternity. See I lead all things to the end I have prepared for them. I do this by the same wisdom and love and power through which I made them. How can anything be done that is not well done?

God wants us to know that he keeps us safe through good and ill.

We shall see God face to face, simply and wholly.

A fifteenth-century Irish poet, Tadhg Óg Ó hUiggin

It is Thou who makest the sun bright, together with the ice; it is Thou who createdst the rivers and the salmon all along the river.

That the nut-tree should be flowering, O Christ, it is a rare craft: through Thy skill too comes the kernel, Thou fair ear of our wheat.

Though the children of Eve ill deserve the bird-flocks and the salmon, it was the Immortal One on the cross who made both the salmon and the birds.

It is He who makes the flower of the sloe grow through the bark of the blackthorn, and the nut-flower on other trees; beside this what miracle is greater?

An African Creed

We believe in the one High God, who out of love created the beautiful world and everything good in it. He created man and wanted man to be happy in the world. God loves the world and every nation and tribe on the earth. We have known this High God in the darkness, and now we know him in the light. God promised in the book of his word, the bible, that he would save the world and all the nations and tribes.

THE QUESTION OF GOD

We believe that God made good his promise by sending his son, Jesus Christ, a man in the flesh, a Jew by tribe, born poor in a little village, who left his home and was always on safari doing good, curing people by the power of God, teaching about God and man, showing that the meaning of religion is love. He was rejected by his people, tortured and nailed hands and feet to a cross, and died. He lay buried in the grave, but the hyenas did not touch him, and on the third day, he rose from the grave. He ascended to the skies. He is the Lord.

We believe that all our sins are forgiven through him. All who have faith in him must be sorry for their sins, be baptized in the Holy Spirit of God, live the rules of love and share the bread together in love, to announce the good news to others until Jesus comes again. We are waiting for him. He is alive. He lives. This we believe. Amen.

Abide with us, Lord, for it is toward evening and the day is far spent. Abide with us and with thy whole Church. Abide with us in the end of the day, in the end of our life, in the end of thy world. Abide with us in thy grace and bounty, with the holy Word and sacrament, with thy comfort and blessing. Abide with us when comes the night of affliction and fear, the night of doubt and temptation, the night of bitter death. Abide with us and with all thy faithful ones, O Lord, in time and in eternity.

(Lutheran Church)

TWO

*

Prayer: The Church's Banquet

I CAN'T BE alone in the fact that over the years certain texts, prayers, and stories have become part of the furniture of my mind. They constitute a sort of 'second canon'—words and images committed to memory, carrying authority, shaping the kind of person I am and hope to become. I have always been moved by a brief passage in the final chapter of Dom Gregory Dix's marvellous book *The Shape of the Liturgy*.[1] There he tells of an ill-spelled epitaph found in Asia Minor during the fourth century. The inscription reads: 'Here sleeps the blessed Chione, who has found Jerusalem for she prayed much.'

The poignancy of the text for me lies partly in the awareness that nothing else is known about Chione—she was probably an obscure woman belonging to a village church in the now vanished world of Christian Anatolia. But sixteen centuries on we know that she prayed much—so much so that others became convinced that the Heavenly City was already her possession. In some ways she is more important to me than the saints and martyrs for she represents all those faithful lives that left no indelible mark on this world and were soon forgotten. Yet beyond doubt as Dix notes: 'Each one of them once believed and prayed as I believe and pray, and found it hard and grew slack and sinned and repented and fell again. Each of them found their thoughts wandering and felt heavy and unresponsive.'

The solidarity I feel with Chione and the great anonymous band of witnesses arises from a shared sense that prayer matters—matters so much that in ways we may not readily acknowledge we actually begin to die a little through our disinclination to attend to it. All of us who have tried to pray know about the besetting distractions, the difficulty we have in switching off, the never-ending list of things that might more profitably engage our energies than this time alone with God. These pitfalls are well documented in the history of the Church: St Benedict talked about 'murmuring' as a kind of cramp or spasm that gets into the soul and turns prayer into conversation with ourselves instead of God. Far from being an adventure or a source of renewal, our praying can become a tiresome traffic in images of self-worth. Hardly surprising, perhaps, in an age which positively endorses the nurturing of self-image—of how one is coming across and the impression being made on others—but, sadly, quite uncongenial once we realize that the purpose behind our praying is to think less about ourselves, not more. Another great teacher on the spiritual life, St Teresa of Avila, is quite unsentimental on this point: 'The first thing we have to do is to still the fool in the house.'

To think less of ourselves is not an invitation to indulge in self-remorse or, worse still, disgust. A healthy awareness of personal failure or inadequacy is a world removed from a morbid preoccupation with the minor faults that constitute our humanity. I rather like the following verse; it is not part of my 'second canon' but the lightness of touch appeals:

> Once in a saintly passion
> I cried with desperate grief,
> 'O Lord my heart is black with guile,
> Of sinners I am chief.'
> Then stopped my guardian angel
> And whispered from behind:
> 'Vanity, my little man;
> You're nothing of the kind'.[2]

If we are going to spend time on our knees or in quietness we need a sense of proportion. Even though our faults 'are ever before us' we can tolerate them once we have accepted the fact that we are accepted by God. This is an old truth, but we have to learn the things which we have known the longest. Or, as that wise and vulnerable Christian gentleman Dr Samuel Johnson once remarked: 'In matters of religion we need to be not so much informed as reminded.' And when, as sometimes happens, a familiar truth strikes us with a fresh vivacity it may owe something to the abiding power of revelation which can take us unawares, or simply that we have made an effort to take the familiar to heart in order to be changed by it.

Whatever prayer is, at its best it calls for the sort of commitment normally associated with religious vows, marriage, or lifelong friendships. Determination, obedience, devotion, and discipline—not least when it all seems 'a day too much'. Prayer is work. It is a duty borne out of desire—whether for God in himself, or for guidance on the road we have still to travel.

This should not surprise us. If genius is 'an infinite capacity for taking pains' the invitation to be perfect[3] which lies at the heart of the Christian life surely demands something costly from us by way of response. This will entail more than learning techniques and methods or absorbing the wide range of books and tapes readily available on the subject of prayer. What we may actually find is that any one of these can become a means of avoiding the real thing—prayer itself and the effort that draws us into it.

I have to say, by way of confession, that I have not always believed this. Twenty years ago I might easily have said a loud 'Amen' to a comment made by Bishop John Robinson who, when reflecting on his own earlier life, recalled a period when the only kind of prayer that made sense was the sort that 'dragged one to one's knees'. In our need, or in our recognition of the needs of others, we find ourselves compelled to utterance.

This was the experience of Brian Keenan, the Irish lecturer kidnapped by fundamentalist Shiite militiamen, and held captive in Beirut for four and a half years. Although not a conventional believer, Keenan's time in captivity reads like a modern

Passion narrative. In the emptiness and unremitting awfulness of the early stages of his ordeal, Keenan and his cell mate John McCarthy 'prayed unashamedly, making no outward sign. We simply knew that each of us did pray and would on occasion remind each other to say a prayer for someone in particular among our families and lovers.'[4]

Prayer is presented here as an elemental part of the human condition—a plea made by all those who descend into various forms of hell and seek solace. No one could deny the integrity of this form of praying, and many of us will have resorted to it. At the end of our own resources and when hope seems exhausted, we instinctively reach out beyond ourselves to God or whatever might sustain us in our hour of grieving. But prayer in its more comprehensive sense entails more than anguished words. It invites us to enter into a deeper relationship with God so that we may love him 'with all our heart, with all our mind, with all our soul, and with all our strength'.[5]

We have always known this, of course—it lies at the heart of the Jewish and Christian tradition which sees our fulfilment as persons coming only through the right direction of our hearts and desires towards God. What we may be slow to realize, however, is that the endeavour is not for God's sake but our own. It has to do with our becoming human, and how we might respond to the brokenness of our world. And it requires us to see ourselves in a truer light: to concede that we are often ambiguous about loving God; that we acquiesce too easily with shabby desires; that we are quick to forfeit holiness for the main chance (in whatever guise it appears). Prayer finds us out, which may explain our reluctance to take it too seriously.

No special pleading is likely to make us embrace prayer with a greater enthusiasm than before. We have to want to pray: it's that simple and that difficult. Others can help us. I'm not referring here to the examples frequently given in well-meaning sermons. I doubt that many of us today pray better because we have been told that the greatest Christian lives were saturated with prayer. This may actually discourage us when our own experience seems dry by comparison. More promising is what we can actually see about us in the lives of those who are praying with some depth and integrity.

My own desire to pray over the years owes much to others. Etched in my memory forever is the sound of feet upon gravel as my theological contemporaries made their way to chapel early each morning; not always fully awake, sometimes on the last minute, occasionally dishevelled, but there nevertheless—even on the most dreadful winter mornings; quietly assembling after the tolling of the bell to offer their silence and praise to God as morning broke. I still find it an attractive and powerful scene, the more so because of its very ordinariness. Going to chapel was part of the natural rhythm of the day along with visits to the library or dining hall. Prayer was presumed, not forced or endured.

Not everyone can pray at break of day; relatively few will have the privilege of belonging to a religious community. But if we haven't already done so, many of us could explore the possibilities of praying regularly with another person. The right person, of course—someone who is already taking the matter seriously, who we know, perhaps respect, and feel we could get alongside without unease or awkwardness. Prayer doesn't have to be a solitary activity: it can still be deeply personal in the presence of another and will often be enhanced because it is a shared offering. Protestantism with its tremendous emphasis on individual responsibility—each one of us standing alone before our Creator—can easily make the practice of prayer seem needlessly daunting. And most of us are struck by those Gospel scenes where Jesus prays alone in the wilderness, or in Gethsemane, or rises very early in the morning to find solitude.[6]

The point is that this is not the only pattern of prayer available to us. Praying of necessity will often be a solitary activity, and it might even occasionally feel heroic when much is required of us. But prayer should also be natural, relaxed even. Jesus called his followers 'friends', and to pray with someone else over a period of time is to ease our self-imposed burdens, and to accept gladly whatever those moments together have to offer.

On our own we can so easily find ourselves fretting over inessentials—saying the correct words in the right order with whatever decorum is deemed appropriate. Close attention to procedure is important in public worship, but much less so in our personal life where what we say needs to be savoured and taken to heart. Pace is not an issue. We are not striving for results, but asking only that whatever is before us may address us. To linger over a text or to refrain from words altogether if it seems right, and to be able to do either in the presence of another person is to experience prayer at a depth we may not have encountered before.

Experimentation is called for—a preparedness to step outside normal 'custom and practice' (which for most of us means the boundaries of our own particular background) and learn from the hidden wisdom of others. Chione, though dead, lives on in the unspectacular but deeply impressive witness of those in our churches who have come to love silence and are at ease with themselves. They represent the heart of that 'wonderful and sacred mystery' which is the Church of God, and maintain it in truth when it falls prey to worldliness or triviality.[7]

They also provide us with a more gracious understanding of what it actually means to belong to the Body of Christ. When we pray alone or find it hard to pray at all, our intercession and thanksgiving should not be looked on as meagre offerings but as part of the 'Church's banquet'—the rich and unceasing flow of prayer and praise of all God's people. For whatever circumstances we find ourselves in, we never actually pray alone, but always within the household of faith, where 'the voice of prayer is never silent nor dies the strain of praise away.'[8]

Perhaps we are not used to thinking of the Church in this way—as a spiritual and mystical communion of believers transcending the limitations of denomination and dogma. All of us, I suspect, suffer from a parochialism of the mind which habitually identifies the Church and its activities with the building where we dutifully assemble week by week. Too easily the resonances of the words we use in worship elude us, and we are not shaken by the realization that our prayers are offered 'with angels and archangels and with all the company of heaven'.[9] And on earth too we are joined by the monk in his cell; the priest at her prayer desk holding the parish in her heart; communities struggling to keep the faith in spiritual wastelands; friends from a distance holding us and our needs before God; choirs and musicians offering every day the best of their gifts to the Maker of all things. We are part of this 'living stream' and, once we grasp this, our praying, whether in sorrow or joy, has a perspective it may have lacked before.

I find it a disconcerting thought that many of us may have prayed for half a lifetime without a clear sense of what we were doing or the validity of it all. Maybe we presumed that no validation was needed: we were encouraged or instructed to say our prayers and did so diligently, not expecting any great return beyond the simple satisfaction that a duty had been discharged. But even to say our prayers does beg the larger questions already touched upon in this chapter: what are the prayers for, and just how are we diminished as people if we decide that praying actually isn't so important after all?

Part of what I have been trying to say so far suggests that prayer cannot be confined to reciting texts or requests for help; it is instead the engagement of the whole personality in relation to God. Put this way prayer has a feeling of romance about it—intimations of a great cause or adventure which even now can lead women and men to renounce everything the world sets great store by.[10] The romance should not blind us to the hazards or the costly self-giving. Progress in prayer is often blighted, not simply by ignorance of how to proceed but an unwillingness to persevere in the task. All too soon we can fall along the wayside with the sad consequence that the seed in Jesus' parable of the sower has scant opportunity to bear fruit.[11]

Quite why we lose our passion for prayer is interesting in itself. Sometimes it will reflect the overall state of our lives and the pressures we are under. Because we still insist on dividing body and soul in an unhelpful way, it occasionally comes as a genuine surprise to discover that the underlying reason for our spiritual torpor is no sudden loss of interest nor an incipient crisis of faith but something altogether more simple. We are tired—weary with the 'cares of this world'—to the point of exhaustion. And if our bodies are close to collapse we should hardly be amazed if we find it impossible to pray with any purpose.

At such times the remedy will often lie in physical renewal—more sleep, adequate rest, and opportunities for re-creation. The way we treat our bodies is instructive, and St Paul's teaching that our physical frame is the temple of the Spirit of God[12] should remind us of the importance of cherishing the body when the need arises. Loving ourselves a little more may in fact be the only way of releasing the energies we need to bear the burdens of others, especially when they seem unrelenting. And if this means sitting lightly to the discipline of prayer at times we should not worry overmuch; prayer is more than an activity of the mind, and a balanced spiritual life requires a sensible rhythm of eating, sleeping, and relaxing.

Exhaustion is one thing and sin another. Self-knowledge has to teach us that a refusal to take prayer seriously or persevere in it is not always the consequence of strain and stress but our own deliberate fault. We simply can't be bothered. Pride, egoism, vanity, the capacity for resentment, and despair can normally be found in the 'rag and bone shop of the human heart.'[13] They represent the dark side of our nature—what Jung called our 'shadow'—and threaten both our humanity and spiritual growth. In Scripture the heart is the fount of wisdom and of life, but it is also from the heart that wickedness proceeds: 'What comes out of the mouth has its origins in the heart. Murder, adultery, fornication, theft, perjury, slander—these all proceed from the heart and defile a man'.[14]

We are wise not to deceive ourselves on this matter; priests, poets, prophets, and philosophers have never flinched from telling us that we are ragged inside—not wicked and certainly not wretched—but ragged, yes, and in need of attention. Prayer therefore does require 'an ordered and sober life'[15] if it is to address the darkness within us. And so we come back to the importance of self-discipline and a wholesome self-awareness. This is an answer to the question posed earlier concerning the purpose of prayer; it has to do with conversion of life—a commitment to an inner transformation, a continuing pattern of dying and rebirth. Prayer exposes us to the 'fightings and fears within' that can easily consume us, but also makes possible their healing by divine grace. Thomas Merton describes this process in the following way: 'Our real journey in life is interior; it is a matter of growth, deepening, and of an ever greater surrender to the creative action of love and grace in our hearts.'[16]

A choice has to be made here: we can admit the validity of Merton's words yet still refuse to commit ourselves because of indolence, sloth, or fear. The prospect of a new self is attractive, but the cost seems prohibitive, and perhaps it is prudent (if in the end death-dealing) to stay as we are. This is the tragedy of our lives—the gnawing sense (often when it is too late) that options were refused and new vistas left unexplored for the sake of a quiet and shallow existence.

True prayer requires that we risk the confrontation with ourselves because it is necessary to wholeness—to that fullness of life promised by Jesus.[17] Confrontation is a test of our courage and our desire to be changed. Michael Tippett's oratorio *A Child of Our Time* contains the exclamation 'I would know my shadow and my light, so shall I at last be whole.'

To some this way of talking about the life of prayer may seem to owe rather too much to the spirit of the age with its various therapies, all promising the realization of our human potential. But there is a crucial difference: prayer has only one ultimate concern—to conform us to the pattern of Christ, to his selfless obedience and love of others. In so doing we may hope to find our true freedom in service, through proper relationships untainted by the crooked motives of our own hearts. Our praying should lead us to a condition of simplicity, and we draw near to this gracious state to the degree in which we become our true selves, not half-dead and walking a desultory path to the grave but alive and rejoicing in 'the glorious liberty of the children of God'.[18]

The above text is of course from St Paul, who in the contradictions and ambivalences of his own life embodied so much of what I am trying to say about prayer as a 'clothing for the soul divine'.[19] Like most of us Paul was a divided person; his self-knowledge led him to an awareness of his sin to an extent that he was prepared to call himself wretched[20]—and this from the man who St Ambrose described as 'Christ's second eye'. There should be encouragement for us here as we toil with our own inconsistencies while seeking to be faithful to Christ. Paul also knew about the cost of caring. It seems clear from his writings that his pastoral role among those early and fragile Christian communities was both bane and blessing. He was weighed down daily by his 'care of all the churches'.[21]

Yet neither the tensions of his own inner life nor the warring factions within his congregations ever swayed him from the consuming goal of his life. In his own words: 'I have suffered the loss of all things and count them as so much refuse in order that I may gain Christ.'[22] The apostle's sublime hymn to love in 1 Corinthians 13 testifies beyond doubt that, when everything has turned to dust and all earthly passions are spent, love remains—the divine love set forth in the face of Jesus. This love lures us on because it contains the fulfilment of our deepest desires. It also reveals that a fair amount of our agenda as persons aspiring to be pilgrims is sometimes second-rate by comparison. It is not that we always set out to be trivial, wayward, uncaring or self-obsessed; it simply reflects the fact that by nature we are fallen, fallible, reluctant to grasp essentials, and ever so eager for novelty and diversion. We can spend an unprofitable lifetime ignoring or evading these truths, but if we are genuinely concerned to 'measure up to the stature of the fullness of Christ'[23] we need to heed the truth about ourselves. Bishop Joseph Butler, a theologian and philosopher of an earlier age, puts the challenge very neatly: 'Things and actions are what they are, and the consequences of them will be what they will be. Why then should we desire to be deceived?'[24]

If prayer is about depth it is also bound up with acceptance—most immediately concerning ourselves and, by extension, a readiness to face the world in all its baffling complexity and fearful need. St Paul remains relevant to our quest because he never averted his eyes from reality even when it was loathsome. He faced situations that threatened to crush him, and set the stark facts of evil and death against the ultimate reality of God's love. That he was able to do this owed everything to his conversion—not just that unique event on the road to Damascus—but his subsequent and growing awareness of Christ's presence within him so that his energies and imperfections were transfigured by it. We have not begun to understand St Paul or the call to conversion which lies at the heart of our praying until we have grappled with his awesome declaration in Galatians 2.20: 'I have been crucified with Christ; it is no longer I who live but Christ who lives in me; and the life I now live in the flesh I live by faith in the Son of God who loved me and gave himself up for me.' As a text to meditate on there are few to compare with it in the whole of the New Testament. As a prayer which we should like to make our own, however diffidently, it has economy, depth, resonance and truth. And as a testimony to the one who died upon the cross, it reminds us that in him is to be found the true meaning of our life. Prayer fails if it does not move us 'into another intensity'[25]—to a more genuine understanding of ourselves untrammelled by illusion or deceit, and to a more compassionate engagement with life. Not, we should note, the sort of 'shallow secular activism' that a former Archbishop of Canterbury[26] rightly castigated as an ersatz form of incarnational faith, but a love of the world that can bear its burdens[27] yet still find grounds for hope and celebration.

Here then is another reason why we pray—to see the world aright and in tune. Refusing, in other words, to settle for the unworthy options of cynicism or withdrawal, and bringing instead a generosity of spirit to the unfinished agenda of human need. And the freedom we enjoy as the children of God will enable us to laugh as we engage in these tasks. It would be odd, after all, not to be amused by ourselves—by the considerable gap between our aspirations and our performance. Prayer enables us to be king and jester in our own private court. And in adversity it may even allow us to smile, for the essential truth has already been grasped that Christ is risen and God reigns.

We have yet to show what the absence of prayer entails for our lives. By this we are not referring to the 'dry' periods when perhaps for good reasons we find praying difficult, but the persistent refusal to commit ourselves because the task does not seem to pay the sort of dividends we can readily appropriate. J. Montgomery's hymn 'Lord teach us how to pray aright' begins the second verse with the line: 'We perish if we cease from prayer.' 'Perish' is a strong word and it might seem to overstate the case. Thousands, perhaps millions, of lives seem to function without the conscious and disciplined activity we have been considering and there is no evidence to suggest their imminent demise. At another level however— the deeper level we have tried to address in this chapter— how willing are these same lives to take upon themselves, in Shakespeare's phrase, 'the mystery of things'? How ready are they to be hurt, exposed, and open to a world where need implies obligation? Not very willing perhaps, and may never be ready. Even before our middle years a protective carapace begins to grow around us to deaden the world's clamour. We want to be left alone even if it means being less alive. The poet T. S. Eliot speaks for all of us who have succumbed to apathy when he puts these words on the lips of the chorus in *Murder in the Cathedral*:

We do not wish anything to happen.
Seven years we have lived quietly,
Succeeded in avoiding notice,
Living and partly living.
There have been oppression and luxury,
There have been poverty and licence
There has been minor injustice.
Yet we have gone on living,
Living and partly living.[28]

More than likely, a great many of us drift into this state almost without realizing it; apathy is insidious, and we cease to be aware of its deadening effect precisely because our capacity for awareness has been steadily eroded over the years. The condition is a spiritual malaise, and a brief passage in the Letter to the Ephesians seems to diagnose it well: 'They live in the emptiness of their minds, their wits darkened, being estranged from the life which is in God through the incomprehension that is in them through the stony hardness of their hearts. They are those who have ceased to feel.'[29]

This last sentence perturbs me and makes me think that 'perish' might be the right word after all to describe the consequences of not attending to the business of prayer. What seems to be at stake is an adequate definition of what it means to lead a proper life. The religious vision of 'all life in Christ made new' is compelling because it demands the best of us, and prayer is the means to this end. By comparison, lives that simply plod on assuming that there is no best to give, no great purpose to achieve, no issues to claim our compassion—in fact, very little to make a fuss about at all—have slipped imperceptibly from a groove into a grave.

Prayer does make a difference to our lives, and its absence can easily render us dead to the joys and sorrows that are all around us. The Old Testament leaves us in no doubt that the stakes are high: 'Today I offer you the choice of life and death, blessing or curse. Choose life.'[30] Enough has been said by now,

I hope, to suggest something of what we are about when we pray. No one explanation of prayer can ever adequately describe such a multifarious activity. Prayer is the proverbial 'coat of many colours', and definitions are best avoided. What we have tried to do is look at prayer in the interests of truth and love, but in the last resort prayer has to be practised rather than talked about. Some closing remarks, then, about the experience of prayer.

In some respects our praying is akin to other creative activities like poetry, painting, or writing. We set off, in other words, into an unknown territory where anything might happen. The important thing is to start, to be still and, when necessary, to seek solitude. These are the essential prerequisites. 'Arrow prayers' are fine as an expression of our needs and concerns as we engage in the 'daily round and common task', but we are talking here of a readiness to place ourselves in the presence of God in a deliberate, sustained, and disciplined way. And what happens when we do this? Many years ago I was struck by the remark of a Cistercian monk in an enclosed order: 'One spends 99.9 per cent of one's day not in adoration.'[31] This is, of course, quite the opposite of what we might presume—that monks and nuns and maybe clergy are daily 'lost in wonder, love and praise', enjoying an intimate rapport with God not given to less fervent believers. But anyone versed in the life of prayer knows this is not the case. Long hours can be spent with no intense feelings at all. Sometimes our ability to focus on God or others seems to desert us, and we feel like the painter who can do nothing but stare at the empty canvas on his easel, or like the writer numbed by the blank page. Prayer is not a matter of feelings alone; it is the business of sitting down, giving ourselves up to the unknown, and waiting. We are not obliged to think or imagine; we should try to loosen our grip on the paraphernalia that normally clutter our minds, and we must teach ourselves to sit quietly. In the waiting we may find the joy and peace which are the fruits of the Spirit, or the dazzling darkness described by St John of the

Cross—a darkness which dispels any cosy feelings but brings us nevertheless to a truer understanding of our dependence on God alone. Both possibilities depend on us, for 'without us God will not: without us God cannot.'[32] Our job is to put ourselves at his disposal—to allow his grace to increase our wisdom and stature. It is so simple but we frequently perish through neglect of the obvious.

> Jesus confirm my heart's desire
> To work and speak and think for thee
> Still let me guard the holy fire
> And still stir up the gift in me.[33]

FOR REFLECTION

From The Foolishness of God *by* John Austin Baker

Once we have grasped clearly what we are doing when we pray for others, we shall see that the most important requirement by far is inner calmness and tranquility. We are not engaged in creating or producing anything, but in becoming aware of what is already the fact, namely that God is immediately and intimately present both to ourselves and to the ones for whom we are praying. Our task is to hold the awareness of this fact in the still centre of our being, to unite our love for them with God's love, in the quiet but total confidence that he will use our love to help bring about the good in them which we both desire. In technical terms, therefore, intercession is a form of that kind of prayer known as 'contemplation', with the special feature that here we contemplate not God himself but God in his relationship of love towards those whom we also love; and on the basis of our partnership with him we entrust our love into his hands to be used in harness with his own for their benefit.

Teach us, O Father, to trust Thee with life and with death,
And (though this is harder by far)
With the life and death of those that are dearer to us than
    our life.

Teach us stillness and confident peace
In thy perfect will,
Deep calm of soul and content
In what Thou wilt do with these lives Thou hast given,

THE BIG QUESTIONS

Teach us to wait and be still,
To rest in Thyself,
To hush the clamorous anxiety,
To lay in Thine arms all this wealth Thou hast given.

Thou lovest these souls that we love
With a love as far surpassing our own
As the glory of noon surpasses the gleam of a candle.
Therefore will we be still,
And trust in Thee.

(J. S. Hoyland)

From Selected Poems 1946–68 *by* R. S. Thomas

KNEELING

Moments of great calm
Kneeling before an altar
of wood in a stone church
In summer, waiting for the God
To speak: the air a staircase
For silence; the sun's light
Ringing me, as though I acted
A great rôle. And the audience
Still; all that close throng
Of spirits waiting, as I,
For the message.
        Prompt me, God;
But not yet. When I speak,
Though it be you who speak
Through me, something is lost.
The meaning is in the waiting.

PRAYER

Isaiah 40.31, Authorized Version

But they that wait upon the Lord shall renew their strength;
they shall mount up with wings as eagles; they shall run,
and not be weary; and they shall walk, and not faint.

Lord, make us the instruments of thy peace;
    Where there is hatred, let us sow love;
    Where there is injury, pardon;
    Where there is doubt, faith;
    Where there is despair, hope;
    Where there is sadness, joy;
    Where there is darkness, light.
Grant that we may not seek so much
    to be consoled, as to console;
    to be understood, as to understand;
    to be loved, as to love;
For in giving we receive, in pardoning we are pardoned,
    and in dying we are born into eternal life.

(St Francis of Assisi)

Teach us, good Lord, to serve thee as thou deservest; to give,
and not to count the cost; to fight and not to heed the
wounds; to toil and not to seek for rest; to labour and not to
ask for any reward save the joy of knowing that we do thy will.

(Ignatius Loyola)

God be in my head,
And in my understanding;
God be in my eyes,
And in my looking;

God be in my mouth,
And in my speaking;
God be in my heart,
And in my thinking;
God be at mine end,
And at my departing.

(fifteenth century)

Christ has no body now on earth but yours, no hands but yours, no feet but yours; yours are the eyes through which is to look out Christ's compassion to the world, yours are the feet with which he is to go about doing good, and yours are the hands with which he is to bless us now.

(St Teresa of Avila)

O God, who art the light of the minds that know thee, the life of the souls that love thee, and the strength of the wills that seek thee, help us so to know thee that we may truly love thee, so to love thee that we may fully serve thee, whose service is perfect freedom; through Jesus Christ our Lord.

(Gelasian Sacramentary)

O God of unchangeable power and eternal light, look favourably on thy whole church, that wonderful and sacred mystery; and by the tranquil operation of thy perpetual providence, carry out the work of our salvation; and let the whole world feel and see that things which were cast down are being raised up, that those things which had grown old are being made new, and that all things are returning to perfection through him from whom they took their origin, even through our Lord Jesus Christ.

(Gelasian Sacramentary)

PRAYER

Preserve us, O Lord, while waking, and guard us while sleeping, that awake we may watch with Christ, and asleep we may rest in peace.

(Roman Breviary)

Thanks be unto thee, our Lord Jesus Christ: for all the benefits which thou hast given us; for all the pains and insults which thou hast borne for us. O most merciful Redeemer, friend and brother: may we know thee more clearly, love thee more dearly, and follow thee more nearly, now and ever.

(St Richard of Chichester)

THREE

*

Let in the Dark: The Love of God and the World's Pain

WHATEVER STRENGTH AND purpose we derive from faith in God and the practice of prayer, both are severely challenged by the problems of evil and innocent suffering. We praise God for his goodness, yet no sooner have the words left our lips than doubt is ready to insert the knife. Disquiet arises because we know as a matter of fact that children die from cruel disorders, that promising lives are robbed of their potential, and bad things happen to good people. Natural disasters if not commonplace are by no means unusual, and Nature though beautiful is also savagely indifferent. We could, if required, go on to speak of human wickedness in all its manifestations—the deliberate human choices that lead to cruelty, lies, theft, and murder. But the point is already made with sufficient force: life is manifestly not perfect, and to be human is to be prey to misfortune. The world as we experience it produces much pain which, in the strict sense, is not our fault. In fact it is no one's fault, unless we are committed to a God who holds this world in being. And there's the rub: for even when we have acknowledged that life holds many pleasures for us, and that our earth is undeniably a beautiful place, why does God permit so much misery? 'Why', the question runs, 'are there so many victims of undeserved suffering in a world created (so we believe) by an all-powerful and good God?' The problem of evil, for believers, is fundamentally a problem for the understanding.

'Why'—wanting the reason 'why', we should note—is an ancient question that can be traced back to the Greek philosopher, Epicurus (*c*.341–270 BC). Since then, many hearts and minds have wrestled with the dilemma which in our own time has assumed a new poignancy with the monstrous evil witnessed in the events of the European Holocaust. We are concerned here not so much with the scale and extent of suffering but the appalling fact that so many who died in the death camps were devout Jews and Christians. They were upright and God-fearing, delighting in his laws and fashioning their lives upon them. They went to their deaths as adherents to religious traditions that affirmed God's goodness (especially to those he called—his chosen ones), and his absolute sovereignty over history and creation. Why, then, did all the rabbis and the faithful die? Or, to put the question another way—where was God in Auschwitz?

To address either question is to engage in the task of theodicy. The term was apparently first coined by the seventeenth-century philosopher, Gottfried Leibniz. 'Theodicy' is derived from the Greek words for God and justice, and may therefore be regarded as the attempt to defend or justify God's power and goodness in the face of suffering. In other words, a belief in a good and loving God may be sustained even in the face of tragedies and the anguish they bring in their train. Suffering, as we know, entails more than physical affliction; it has to do with the awareness of abandonment and loneliness that can be observed, for example, in the 'psalms of lament'.[1] We can learn there of illness and physical pain, but the afflicted also speak of dissolution, depicted with words like 'pour out' and 'empty'. And alongside the psalms we have one of the most extraordinary individuals in the Hebrew Scriptures: the tormented figure of Job, in the book named after him which centres around the specific issues of why a righteous and upright man suffers.

Those familiar with the story will recall that despite Job's impeccable credentials as a God-fearing man of blameless life he falls prey to a string of unmerited calamities culminating in running sores from head to foot. Following a period of self-imposed silence and having been reduced to a state of wretchedness, he finally curses the day he was born and, significantly, finds no comfort at all in the religious answers proffered by his three friends as they try to justify his predicament. We know that by the end of the book Job is a chastened man; his legitimate grievances are ultimately inconsequential in the light of God's answer:

> Then Job answered the Lord: I know that thou canst do all things and that no purpose is beyond thee. But I have spoken of great things which I have not understood, things too wonderful for me to know. I knew of thee only by report, but now I see with mine own eyes. Therefore I melt away and repent in dust and ashes.[2]

Despite his final submission, Job remains a noble figure; his refusal throughout the story to be consoled by the conventional piety of his onlookers is derived from his understanding of the nature and purposes of a good God. Undeserved pain is one thing, but that God should seem to act in a way that is out of keeping with his essential character is, for Job, both a bewildering mystery and a matter for lament. In short, his sense of God as merciful, just, and true will simply not allow him to accept that God could be party to human woe and not do anything.

More often than we might wish, we have to contend with decent folk who, like Job, are stunned and sometimes outraged when disasters beset them. They are at a loss to understand and they are desperate for an answer. What are we to say? Words of consolation may easily become platitudes and simply add to the bewilderment of those who suffer. They feel we are not answering their difficulties, and their grievance is genuine. We do sometimes prattle on to no good effect. And occasionally we display pastoral insensitivity—an inability to tread softly on the holy ground of pain. The mother whose baby has just died at birth will not be helped by the chirpy remark that 'she will soon get over her little disappointment'. What she actually needs from us is not a torrent of words—savaged by the writer E. M. Forster as 'poor, little, talkative Christianity'—but the sort of reticence that respects the depth of her loss. Scripture is helpful at this point: the writer of Ecclesiastes reminds us that 'there is a time for speech and a time for silence'.[3] We might also recall that when the friends of Job came to him in his distress, seven days and nights passed before they spoke a word. They sat beside him on the ground, 'for they saw that his suffering was very great'.[4] In our own time, as Jewish thinkers surveyed the aftermath of the Holocaust some insisted that the only possible stance in the light of such unspeakable acts was that of silence. A text hallowed by Jewish tradition is: 'And Aaron was silent.'[5]

So we need to choose our words carefully and when appropriate refrain from them altogether. Another temptation to avoid is the morally dodgy notion that when sorrows come upon us they are sent to try us. We can and often do learn through adversity, but few are ennobled by destructive pain and many are broken. It has to be recognized that, although the Holocaust gave rise to countless acts of heroism and faith, some went to their deaths in the conviction that they had been abandoned by God, and consequently no longer believed in him.

When to speak and when to be silent depends upon 'discernment'—that precious pastoral gift which comes from a sound moral sense and a readiness at times to admit the inadequacy (at one level) of our answer. Without contradicting anything we have just said we should also wish to say that on certain occasions true religion is not always best served by a deferential silence. This could, unwittingly, give rise to the notion that we believe in a vindictive God—a divine despot who will tolerate no questioning of his ways on the part of his subjects. St Paul comes close to this view when he represents human beings as 'lumps of clay in the potter's hand'.[6] But if our freedom and dignity are to mean anything at all we must be free to question God's purposes. A faith which cannot speak openly of suffering and death and the profound issues they raise is hardly a faith worth having. Crucifixion ripped the most desperate question of all from the lips of Jesus[7] and since then Jobs without number have taken issue with God. Some Jewish thinkers found it impossible to pass by the horrors of Auschwitz and Treblinka in silence, and argued that survivors had a religious responsibility to reason with God, and if need be to wrestle with him.[8] They recalled that, in the book of Genesis, Abraham confronted God concerning the fate of Sodom and Gomorrah, challenging him to do right by the inhabitants of the city.[9] Their attempt to understand God's providence in the death camps was therefore in keeping with the biblical tradition.

So far we have established that evil of one sort or another exists in sufficient measure to place a caveat against traditional religious teaching concerning an omnipotent and benevolent God. Moreover, evil is unmistakably real with a terrifying power all of its own. Cruelty and hatred are not indications of the absence of kindness and love. They exist in their own right as painful intrusive realities, and as such often present a serious obstacle to those who would like to believe in a good God but cannot. The evidence, in their estimation, seems to point in the opposite direction, making the world seem at best a deeply ambiguous place where we can be overwhelmed at any moment. An omnipotent God should, frankly, be able to organize things better, thereby eliminating or at least minimizing much in life that seems so arbitrary and capricious and inimical to our well-being.

On the surface this seems a reasonable presumption, but on reflection we can see that it gives no weight at all to what in a Christian view of things is of striking importance—our capacity to act as moral agents. Just for a moment let us consider what the implications might be in a world custom-made for the avoidance of all suffering. In his book, *Evil and the God of Love*, John Hick comments that in such a world:

no wrong action could ever have bad effects. . . . no ill judgement could ever lead to harmful consequences. If a thief were to steal a million pounds from a bank, instead of anyone being made poorer thereby, another million pounds would appear from nowhere to replenish the robbed safe. If one man tried to murder another, his bullet would melt innocuously into thin air or the blade of his knife turn to paper.[10]

Hick provides many more examples, and arrives at the daunting conclusion that in a pain-free world moral qualities would no longer have any significance or purpose. A world which denies the possibility of love and devotion, honesty and courage would be a place where these qualities, and many other virtues, would never come into being. Truthfulness, perseverance, trust, and self-sacrifice would be redundant. Moral character formed through free, responsible thought and action lies at the heart of our humanity, and to be a person is to have the choice to act well or badly. Even God cannot give individuals free will and the opportunity of exercising it, of choosing good and rejecting evil, if they are placed in a world in which there is no evil, and therefore, no possibility of choice. It seems that we have to accept the inevitability of risk if we wish to speak of ourselves as persons with the freedom to choose.

We inhabit a world where a good and powerful God permits the possibility of moral evil—everything from the calculated abuse of a child to the heinous extremities of a Stalin. Not to permit this would so diminish our freedom as individuals as to reduce us to the level of automata. This would admittedly vouchsafe to us a safer and more agreeable environment, but it would then hardly make sense, morally speaking, to regard ourselves as moral agents any longer. Furthermore, a totally pleasant life devoid of suffering and misery would not be a human life (as we understand it), for it would necessarily lack most, if not all, of the human qualities that we find most admirable.

If, momentarily, we were able to assume God's point of view, with the authority to choose the kind of world best suited to our nature, what choice would we make? A world in which there are great moral struggles and the possibility of wonderful triumphs and the inevitability of many defects; or a world in which there are less intense struggles, less amazing triumphs and fewer defects; or a world in which there are no struggles, no triumphs, and no defects?[11] It is logically possible for individuals to be imbued with a nature such that they always freely do the right thing in an hedonistic environment where hurts never intrude. But would we relish the prospect of living in such a world, where genuine freedom, moral character, and the pursuit of virtue would be meaningless terms? It does seem that our weaknesses and the negative side of human life constitute the soil in which virtues grow. A good deal of what we find most admirable involves to some extent an acceptance of suffering and the overcoming of evil. Of course, we do what we can to eliminate suffering, but there is wisdom in the acceptance of its inevitability and the realization of its curious contribution to our growth as free persons. Critics of this view would presumably argue that the cost of freedom and moral growth is simply too high if, as for example in the case of the Holocaust, it entails atrocities on a scale that may suggest freedom itself (in its fullest sense) is a morally dubious gift. But what they would offer presumably in place of our precarious world is the sort of sybaritic existence that we have already rejected on the moral grounds that it is not recognizably human. Our values and aspirations are such that we could not thrive in world where we would effectively be little better than well-fed pigs wallowing in a trough. The essential point is that we are not pigs; we are persons.

In acknowledging the difficulty of imagining a worth-while existence without suffering and evil we have still to explain why things are as they are—why there is so much gratuitous suffering, and why it leads many sensitive minds to conclude that there is neither justice nor a judge in the universe. We could at this point with some justification opt for silence, and concede that the mystery of suffering is unfathomable, and challenges us, no less than our critics, with its baffling meaninglessness. A robust answer to the problem of needless pain is simply not available and, like Job, we have to reckon with an inscrutable God whose ways and thoughts are beyond our understanding. The religious mind can perhaps learn to live with this uncertainty, but sceptics are unlikely to be persuaded on the grounds that if this is the best answer we can muster it is unbelievably tenuous and thin. To keep the dialogue open we might ask the doubters to elaborate a little on their actual understanding of God—particularly with regard to the extent of his power. By way of reply it is quite likely that they will say that God by virtue of his power and wisdom should be able to do anything. Nothing should be outside his control.

What comes to mind here is the clockmaker model of God popularized in the eighteenth century[12] whereby the world was set going long ago by the creator who then let it run according to its own laws and mechanisms. This crudely mechanistic interpretation of the universe simply does not fit our current understanding of the creation. The scientist and theologian John Polkinghorne has written of 'a world with ragged edges where order and disorder interlace with each other, and where the exploration of possibility by chance will lead not only to the evolution of systems of increasing complexity, but also the evolution of systems imperfectly formed and malfunctioning.'[13] On this view the world is still being made. Far from being a finished product in all respects perfect, the 'whole creation groaneth and travaileth in pain'[14] (to borrow an insight from St Paul). Properly understood, the creative activity of God is to be seen as a continuing 'labour of love'. Omnipotence, then, is not about total control but the possibility of risk—of things coming right or coming wrong. If this is so then the existence of evil must be seen as the consequence of the precariousness of divine creativity. In his compelling and award-winning book *Love's Endeavour Love's Expense* the Anglican theologian William Vanstone comments:

If the creation is the work of love, then its shape cannot be predetermined by the Creator, nor its triumph foreknown. . . . each step is a precarious step into the unknown, in which each triumph contains new potential of tragedy, and each tragedy may be redeemed into a wider triumph. . . . The creation is 'safe' not because it moves by programme towards a predetermined goal but because the same loving creativity is ever exercised upon it.[15]

By way of analogy, Vanstone describes the self-giving of God in creation with an eyewitness account of an operation observed in a London hospital:

It was the first time that this particular brain operation had been carried out in this country. It was performed by one of our leading surgeons upon a young man of great promise for whom after an accident there seemed to be no other remedy. It was an operation of the greatest delicacy in which a small error would have had fatal consequences. In the outcome the operation was a triumph but it involved seven hours of intense and uninterrupted concentration on the part of the surgeon. When it was over, the nurse had to take him by the hand, and lead him from the operating theatre like a blind man or a little child.[16]

Here we are being asked to see creation as a work of redemption—the task of 'winning back' which is ever present in the risk of divine creativity. God is not some imperious monarch detached from his handiwork but One who is passionately engaged in the costly business of integrating that which has gone wrong into the overall divine purpose. Anyone who has ever created anything of worth will be aware of this struggle—of finding a way by which imperfection or error can be made to contribute to the total vision rather than frustrate or impoverish it. Divine control, then, will not necessarily prevent the wrong—earthquakes, floods, and cancers will persist because that's the way the world is—but it will seek to redeem it. This is the hallmark of God's love. His power does not consist in the ability to do anything, but rather in terms of his power to love all creation—'even to the edge of doom'.[17]

We are a long way from Sunday school images of God as the One who 'has the whole world in his hands'. Our world is not some plaything—a pleasing bauble in the hands of the Almighty. It is a costly, precarious thing calling forth from God that unceasing endeavour which requires us to see him as a fellow-sufferer rather than an amused spectator.

All of this may strike us as disconcerting and difficult, but is it really so far removed from the knowledge of God that we derive from the scriptural image of Christ? In his letter to the Philippians, St Paul reminds us in striking terms that God in the form of Christ 'emptied himself taking the form of a servant . . . and became obedient unto death, even death on a cross'.[18] With all the power of mind and imagination that we possess we need to grasp (however tenuously) what is being intimated here. When the crucified Jesus is called 'the image of the invisible God'[19] the meaning is that this is God, and God is like this. Writing of the cross, the German theologian Jürgen Moltmann comments:

> God is not greater than he is in this humiliation. God is not more powerful than he is in this helplessness. God is not more divine than he is in this humanity. The nucleus of everything that Christian theology says about God is to be found in this Christ event.[20]

Moltmann's concern is to demonstrate that at the deepest point of human extremity it may be affirmed that God is for us and with us. In Christ he too suffers pain and takes death into himself. That God the maker of all things could be exposed to disaster, dereliction, and death in this way will be for some, perhaps, a shocking thought. The more so if we have been led to believe that change and decay cannot affect the unchangeable power and eternal might of our Creator. Sadly, hymns and sermons alike sometimes contain bad theology. To dig only a little into the treasure trove that is church history is to discover that eminent and orthodox theologians had no qualms in identifying absolutely the suffering and death of Christ with God himself. Tertullian, a second-century Christian author, speaks of the suffering of God and even of the 'dead God'. Others talk of the 'crucified God', or say that 'God suffered'. Logic rather than speculation brought them to this conclusion. In short, suffering could not be restricted simply to the humanity of Christ without neglecting or abandoning the unity of the person of Christ with God to which Scripture and later teaching testified.[21]

Where this theological excursion is leading us to is the recognition that although we do not have an answer to the world's pain we may have the beginning of an answer. Argument alone will bring scant illumination to those who walk in darkness or the valley of the shadow of death. But they may find hope and meaning in the cross of Christ as God's act of loving solidarity with all the wretched and tormented of the world. A modern hymn expresses this well:

> And when human hearts are
> breaking
> Under sorrow's iron rod,
> Then they find that self-same aching
> Deep within the heart of God[22]

It may be argued that another person's suffering of itself does little or nothing to diminish the tragedy of an individual's suffering, even if, as we have suggested, the other is God himself. Our response to this is to look again at the form of Jesus' death—especially its arbitrariness. Had he been born centuries earlier in another place he could, like the philosopher Socrates, have taken the painless way out—a cup of hemlock dutifully imbibed at the designated hour. But instead he submits to that most perturbing aspect of suffering, its essential arbitrariness. There is no providential reason why some die in their prime and others breathe their last full of years; no reason why Mother Teresa of Calcutta is acclaimed by all while another heroic believer pines away in a Soviet psychiatric hospital, forgotten even by fellow Christians. It is this which makes Christ's cry of dereliction from the cross the lament of all sufferers: 'Why me?' Why has God abandoned me to this fate? In Jesus we see God himself endorsing the cry of all new sufferers as they discover for themselves that there is no reason why misfortune has afflicted them instead of another.

Jesus goes to the cross a failure: to the Jewish authorities he appears a blasphemer; to the Romans a common criminal; to his own disciples a visible testimony that the hope of the coming kingdom was a chimera. Dying, he finds himself abandoned by almost everyone (save the women at the foot of the cross). Yet we come to see that despite the apparent randomness of Jesus' death, meaning is evident in it and good comes out of it. The centurion watching Jesus die is moved to comment: 'Truly, this man was the Son of God.'[23] There must have been something in the manner of Jesus' dying to prompt this remark. We might recall that the anguished cry: 'My God, my God why has thou forsaken me?' is in fact the opening verse of Psalm 22 which ends on a note of confidence and trust. And there can be little doubt that in St John's account of the crucifixion we are compelled to see it as an achievement. 'It is finished'[24] is not the cry of a man capitulating to wickedness but an affirmation that a redeeming work has been accomplished. God in Christ enters the worst pain of all, the pain of meaninglessness and affords it a meaning. If then we are moved to speak of divine assistance helping us creatively to transform whatever befalls us now, the source of our help flows from one who knew pain at its worst and potentially most destructive.[25]

There is no final guarantee that ourselves or others shall be protected from the accidents and ills of this life. That this should be so is due, as we have argued, to the sort of power that God extends over his world. In the end omnipotence is not about the tight control of a computer programme over the operation of a machine. Rather the benevolent power in which we trust is best expressed in terms of the constancy and reliability of God. Amidst the 'changes and chances of this fleeting world' which render us subject to microbes, viruses, and death, we are held within the 'eternal changelessness' of a love that bears and endures all things. Among these we must also include the greed, wickedness, and cruelty that can arise from the choices we make. Like the world itself, human freedom is a risky business, at once shaping the kind of moral persons we become and to some extent restricting the divine initiative in our lives. But this it seems is the way of God. His love does not coerce. Force is not an attribute of love.

We are probably wise to say little more than this. Much, as a consequence, is necessarily left unresolved. To the possible rejoinder that we have not dealt adequately with our original question: 'Where was God in Auschwitz?' we can justifiably put the question another way, and ask instead: 'Where was humanity in Auschwitz?' Half a century on, we have still to make sense of the malignant energies at work in the death camps—the rituals of derision, the obscenities and degradations implemented with such banal efficiency. The profound issues they raise challenge our pretensions to humane and civilized behaviour just as much as they question the presence of God in a human hell of our own devising.

There is one more thing to say. It concerns the hope of heaven where: 'there shall be no more death, neither sorrow nor crying, neither shall there be any more pain: for the former things are passed away.'[26] We cannot easily relinquish this hope, offering as it does the final vindication of God's love. Let us be clear: the extremity of evil and suffering are such that nothing less than this ultimate vision of human redemption can do justice to the Christian notion that if there is a God he is a God of love. In this sense, we can say that if God is to be true to his essential nature he is morally obliged to raise the dead. Only if all the innocent sufferers are offered the hope of heaven, can there be any real justification for asserting both the goodness of God and the value of human life in a world where things fall apart with disarming ease.

Without a belief in a hereafter the moral case against God is overwhelming, and as Stendhal tersely remarked: 'The only excuse for God would be for him not to exist.'[27] How we are to understand the idea of heaven in a sceptical age like ours where angels are only to be encountered on hospital wards takes us appropriately to the next chapter.

FOR REFLECTION

Hear me and answer
for my cares give me no peace
I am panic stricken at the shouts of my enemies
at the shrill clamour of the wicked.
My heart is torn with anguish
and the terrors of death come upon me
and I shudder from head to foot

(Psalm 55.2–5, NEB)

The people were still standing like columns of stone with no room to fall or lean. Even in death you could tell the families all holding hands. It was difficult to separate them while emptying the room for the next batch. The bodies were tossed out, blue, wet with sweat and urine, the legs smeared with excrement and menstrual blood. Two dozen workers were busy checking mouths they opened with iron hooks. Dentists knocked out gold teeth, bridges and crowns with hammers.

(Eye witness account of the killings at Belzec cited by Dan Cohn-Sherbok in *Holocaust Theology* (Lamp Press, 1989), p. 8)

God was in Christ reconciling the world to himself.

(2 Cor. 5.19)

LET IN THE DARK

In the end we see the power, the wisdom, the presence of God in terms of his love and compassion: something that could never have been so apart from the incarnation.

(Rt. Revd Peter Walker, article
Church Times, 24.12.92)

God is Christ-like, and in him there is no un-Christlikeness at all.

(Michael Ramsey, Archbishop of Canterbury,
1961–1974)

There is only one way in which, with the world as it is, God can show himself good in respect of man's suffering; and that is by not asking of us anything that he is not prepared to endure himself. He must share the dirt and the sweat, the bafflement and loneliness, the pain, the weakness, yes, and the death too. That would be a God one could respect, a God who put aside all his magic weapons and did it all as one of us.

(John Austin Baker)

O Lord we pray thee for all weighed down with the mystery of suffering. Reveal thyself to them as the God of love who thyself doest bear all sufferings. Grant that they may know that suffering borne in fellowship with thee is not waste or frustration, but can be turned to goodness and blessing greater than if they had never suffered, through him who on the cross suffered rejection and hatred, loneliness and despair, agonising pain and physical death, and rose victorious from the dead, conquering and to conquer, even Jesus Christ our Lord.

(George Appleton)

THE BIG QUESTIONS

Jesus our brother,
you followed the necessary path
and were broken on our behalf.
May we neither cling to our pain
where it is futile,
nor refuse to embrace the cost
when it is required of us;
that in losing our selves for your sake,
we may be brought to new life,
Amen

(Janet Morley)

Christ our victim,
whose beauty was disfigured
and whose body torn upon the cross;
open wide your arms
to embrace our tortured world,
that we may not turn away our eyes,
but abandon ourselves to your mercy,
Amen

(Janet Morley)

FOUR

*

Heaven: A Sure and Certain Hope?

THE PLACE IS a windswept cemetery on a cold December afternoon. The light is already beginning to fade as a small group of mourners assembles in a garden of remembrance. A priest carefully scatters the ashes of a tiny baby. Prayers are said and there are the inevitable tears of loss. To mark the spot there is a newly inscribed plaque which reads simply 'SAFE IN THE ARMS OF JESUS'. The words have been chosen by the grandmother, and they seem to ease the pain a little. Muted farewells are exchanged, and the people part.

A similar scene, only now we are in the Wye Valley and the year is 1877. It is Christmas Day early in the afternoon. The Reverend Francis Kilvert, vicar of Bredwardine, records the event in his diary:

> Immediately after dinner I had to go back to the church for the funeral of little Davie who died on Monday. The weather was dreadful, the snow driving in blinding clouds. The Welcome Home, as it chimed softly and slowly to greet the little pilgrim coming to his rest, sounded bleared and muffled through the thick snowy air. The poor father was crying bitterly and the afternoon was very dark. I preached from Luke 2.7 'There was no room for them in the inn' and connected the little bed in the churchyard in which we had laid Davie to rest with the manger cradle at Bethlehem.[1]

The pathos and grief accompanying each scene are quite probably identical, and yet the mourners unquestionably inhabit vastly different worlds. Along with Kilvert, those forlorn figures in the churchyard shared an almost universal belief in an afterlife; where education was concerned it was natural for a cleric to presume that a child's most important need was to be prepared not so much for this life as for eternity. Life for the poor was harsh and often brief but there was always the consolation of heaven beyond this 'vale of tears'. Death was inevitable, but religion drew its sting by portraying it as a gateway to a better place.

A sceptical age like ours no longer seems able to entertain such certainties. Here is Khrushchev gleefully commenting on Gagarin's first space mission in 1961:

> As to paradise in heaven we heard about it from the priests. But we wanted to see for ourselves what it is like, so we sent our scout there Yuri Gagarin. He circled the globe and found nothing in outer space—just complete darkness . . . nothing that looked like paradise.

At one level this is a crass remark. Someone might have tactfully explained to Khrushchev that when Russian icon painters depict heaven, the colour they use is invariably gold not blue— conveying the important insight that whatever paradise is, it should not be confused with the 'spacious firmament on high'.[2]

We take the point however. Our eyes survey the night sky, and we find ourselves in the centre of immensities. Where precisely is heaven in a cosmos without edges? At a loss for explanation or answer and caring little or nothing for the dubious consolations of religion, many have come to the conclusion that death is simply the end—the dissolution of all that we are or might hope to be. Bertrand Russell expressed it succinctly: 'I believe that when I die I shall rot, and nothing of my ego will survive.'[3]

If this life is all we have, would it not then be better to seize the day with all its delights and opportunities, instead of wasting our energies on illusory hopes and unrealistic goals? We can hardly deny that the modern world is in many ways a consumer paradise on earth compared with the squalid conditions endured by earlier generations. Why not just enjoy what we have and leave it at that? J. Prevert's quirky reworking of the Lord's Prayer certainly encourages us in this direction:

Our Father, who art in heaven,
Stay there,
And we will stay here on earth
Which is at times so lovely
With its mysteries of New York
With its mysteries of Paris
Which absolutely outweigh the mystery of the Trinity.[4]

Those with easy access to life's glittering prizes could presumably embrace this transformed rendition of hallowed words as a contemporary creed. Yet for all their loveliness, New York and Paris hardly figure in the hearts and minds of the world's poor whose main preoccupation is the securing of daily bread. The persistent experience of endemic poverty leads the wretched of the earth to pray that God's 'will be done on earth as it is in heaven'. Their suffering makes Prevert's Pater Noster seem at best a clever conceit by comparison.

We are still left with a nagging question however—one that is directly traceable to the writings of Freud.[5] Just suppose that the whole religious enterprise (particularly as it touches the hungry and downtrodden) rests on an illusion. In other words our hope of heaven (and its foretaste here) is a comforting 'projection' with one purpose only—to deny the harsh truths confronting us at every turn. Here is Freud describing the gist of the religious illusion:

Over each of us there watches a benevolent Providence which is only seemingly stern and which will not suffer us to become a plaything of the over-mighty and pitiless forces of nature. Death itself is not extinction, is not a return to inorganic lifelessness, but the beginning of a new kind of existence which lies on the path of development to something higher.[6]

Religion then, properly understood, is, in Freud's estimation, a consoling construction for those who cannot face up to the facts that nature is indifferent to our concerns and death is waiting to consume us in its voracious maw. All of this is unbearable, so we cling desperately to the wreckage of our lives investing them with a spurious significance even as we drown. Better by far that we face the world with a clear eye and recognize the dubious motives behind our beliefs and how insubstantial the world of make-believe is.

It would be churlish to dismiss these views as nothing more than the rantings of an irreligious thinker. Freud was a brave and brilliant man whose writings challenge us to think about self-knowledge and self-deceit. It is generally accepted, however, that he claimed too much on the basis of too little evidence[7] and was mistaken in supposing that his discoveries at the level of psychoanalysis could be regarded as scientific laws. Freud could claim no more authority for his findings than could be asserted for the subjective speculations of anyone else. In fact he was so dogmatic on religious matters that impartial critics have suggested the likelihood of an emotional rather than an objective scientific approach to this area of his work.[8] His useful gift to the life of faith, however, lies in the crucial distinction he enables us to make between hope and what we may call desire.

Perhaps the best description of hope available to us is that recorded by St Paul: 'Things beyond our seeing, things beyond our hearing, things beyond our imagining, all prepared by God for those who love him'.[9] The apostle invites us to trust in God by hoping for a future which is ultimately unknown and beyond the range of our present experience. It is then, literally, a hope for we know not what—if we like, a blank cheque. We should therefore not be too surprised if the object of our hope—in this case heaven—proves to be other than we had imagined.

Much of our difficulty concerning the future life consists in the simple but often unacknowledged fact that we apply to it the logic of desire instead of the logic of hope. We assume that the hereafter will be modelled on what we desire as the people we are now with our present capacity for joy and happiness intensified.

Desire is a counterfeit hope precisely because it trades on our capacity for nostalgia. Unchecked it makes the prospect of life everlasting nothing more than the mirror image of our present state with pleasures intact and blemishes removed. Instead of heaven expressing fulfilment in terms of what has yet to be revealed, we domesticate paradise and view it as the resumption of the way we were without the sorrow and the pain.

This is to fall inevitably into the mode of thinking that Freud so carefully exposed and criticized as 'infantile'. It makes heaven seem either ridiculous or incredible or (following Freud's analysis) 'the projection of our own wishes on to the sky'.[10] We need to guard, then, against mere wishful thinking, and discipline ourselves in relation to the hope that sustains us. This will entail a refusal to cling to the past and a new openness 'to him who is able to do immeasurably more than all we can ask or conceive . . .'[11]

This new way of seeing carries with it important implications. It will shape how we read the New Testament, particularly, for example, those final chapters of the book of Revelation describing 'a city of pure gold . . . adorned with jewels of every kind'.[12] We are not being asked to dispense with this and similar images as the work of a florid imagination, but only to see them for what they are—metaphors, symbols, poetry—all in their different ways pointing to the sacred inexpressible realities which lie beyond themselves.

Like death, heaven is an 'undiscover'd country',[13] and we shall find ourselves on precarious ground (theologically and philosophically) if we persist in the mistaken notion that biblical depictions of heaven are 'the truth, the whole truth and nothing but the truth'. Because heaven is such an elusive concept, even our best images represent an attempt to say something that in the last resort cannot be adequately described. We are confronted by what St Augustine called 'poverty of speech'. If we persist in trying to define something that is too profound for words, we shall only succeed in reducing it to something more shallow.

Learning to watch our language, then, when we read the Bible (or say the Creed) is an important element in our Christian maturity. We shall grow precisely in relation to our ability to see what is going on—in short, what the words and images are actually seeking to convey. So then, if we are asked if the first letter of Peter is true when it says we are saved 'through the resurrection of Jesus Christ who has gone into heaven and is seated at the right hand of God with angels authorities and powers subject to him',[14] we can reply 'yes'. But we shall go on to say that the statement expresses its truth metaphorically and that Scripture is in no way diminished by this admission.

A final point before we move on. We have seen that words are capable of more than one meaning, that study of the Bible involves us all in the difficult work of interpretation. Helping others to see this requires an 'infinite capacity for taking pains' on our part. We shall prove poor stewards of the riches (metaphor again) that have been entrusted to us if we too readily dismiss the beliefs of others as crass, simplistic, and naive. If in conversation or from the privileged space of the pulpit we venture on the subject of heaven, and suggest that we shall not in fact in the end all 'gather at the river, the beautiful, beautiful river' as the gospel chorus promises, we should not be too surprised if we later receive sarcastic thanks for having destroyed someone's faith. Good teaching calls for courtesy and respect towards those whose patterns of belief are different from our own. We can only encourage, in the hope that they will find out the truth for themselves in their own time.

Up to this point we have been trying to clear the ground a little—to remove some of the clutter that hinders our understanding of what we may call ultimate things. Heaven confronts us with a mystery, and we do the cause of true religion no favours if we fail to recognize that the words we use are sometimes a cloak for our ignorance and vain longings. A careful reading of the Gospels will show us that although the afterlife was part of Jesus' teaching, his scattered sayings on the subject do not constitute descriptions. There is a decent reticence in his use of language that should rightly caution us if we are tempted to be a little too precise concerning what lies beyond this life. Jesus seems to favour allusions rather than hard definitions, and they arise in connection with other issues on which he had something significant to say.[15]

Up to a point we can be agnostic about heaven without feeling we are wavering in our faith. Reticence is preferable to brashness and, as we have seen, is consistent with Jesus' own measured approach. Pastorally speaking, it is also surely more effective than the awful gobbledegook we sometimes encounter in church circles which gives outsiders the distinct impression that being a Christian requires them to believe 'six impossible things before breakfast'.[16]

Perhaps, then, it is enough to affirm simply that God will be all in all, and in the meantime we are to get on with the precarious business of living. Modern theology sometimes reflects this new emphasis which insists upon the Christian transformation of this life whether in the form of 'religionless Christianity'[17] or various sorts of 'liberation theology'[18] as our only proper task. A word of caution here. If we sit lightly to heaven or shun the promise of eternal life, are we left anything that is distinguishable from humanism and the passionate concerns of all those who care for the common good without God?

As we noted in the previous chapter, a form of Christianity that seeks to justify its continuing existence solely in terms of serving others must necessarily place the issue of innocent suffering beyond any hope of final resolution. This may be an honourable position for the humanist, but is surely untenable for a faith which from the beginning has asserted the final victory of love over injustice and death.[19]

Being agnostic about heaven does not require us to be dumb. Too much is at stake concerning the integrity of what we claim to believe. We must also reckon with the embarrassment and ignorance that is often evident from 'corner of the mouth' remarks when conversation turns to matters of transcendence. Ours is an age of doubt. Uncertainty is in the air we breathe, and the churches are not immune. We need to speak, not simply to remind ourselves and others that heaven is an important matter (and can we really remain silent about things we cherish most?) but also to help those who may be wrestling with doubts concerning things they no longer believe. What worked in the earlier years may now be of little or no use to the person struggling towards maturity and acutely aware of the need 'to put away childish things'.[20] Consider, for example, the sensitive issue of boredom:

> Father of Jesus, love's reward
> What rapture will it be
> Prostrate before thy throne to lie
> And gaze and gaze on thee.[21]
> (Father Faber, 1814–1863)

The verse is taken from a lovely hymn, and there is no need to doubt the sincerity of the writer whose sentimental creations were the joy of earlier generations. But the picture he paints is hardly enticing, and we could be forgiven for viewing earth (or hell for that matter) as a more promising prospect.

H. H. Price gently but firmly questions the purpose of heaven as endless adoration and singing:

> No doubt the congregation would contain many very admirable persons, and it would be a pleasure, indeed an honour, to be singing in their company. But it did not seem to occur to religious teachers that a perpetual Sunday morning might become tedious after a while. One can have too much of a good thing'.[22]

Not all ethereal images are boring. The poets, mystics, and saints are able to furnish us with timeless intimations that enrich our hopes and speak to our deepest longings. Without needless elaboration they convey the heart of the matter—the conviction that in the end 'all shall be well, and all manner of things shall be well'.[23] Here is a beautiful prayer by John Donne:

> Bring us O Lord God at our last awakening into the house and gate of heaven. To enter into that gate and dwell in that house where there shall be no darkness or dazzling, but one equal light; no noise nor silence but one equal music; no fears nor hopes but one equal possession; no ends nor beginnings but one equal eternity; in the habitation of thy glory and dominion world without end.[24]

It is a deeply satisfying prayer because it has about it what J. B. Phillips once described as 'the ring of truth'. In a way that we cannot easily articulate let alone begin to understand, we are offered a vision that reflects our most profound intuitions touching our human destiny and the loving purposes of a gracious God. The genius of Donne and others like him[25] affords us a vocabulary when we should otherwise be speechless. More importantly, we are brought to the realization that however diffident our speech, our concern in the end is about something and not nothing.

Donne gives us a tantalizing glimpse of a future where activity, creativity, and contemplation are combined in equal measure. We cannot easily say more than this, but once again we are taken beyond a stultifying picture of heaven where 'like stars his children crowned, all in white shall wait around'.[26] 'Will there be anything to do in heaven?' is a legitimate question. By way of an answer much will depend on how we regard the various activities that engage us now. Are we only 'doing' when we are striving for achievement and excellence in our work, or have we learnt to give equal value to reflection and contemplation? 'Be still then and know that I am God'[27] is a perennial reminder that strenuous activity is neither our chief nor final purpose. We pay lip service to this truth yet our frenetic lives often suggest the opposite. The wise discover sooner rather than later the 'real permanent happiness to be found in tranquil contemplation'.[28] This is not to suggest that the only proper life to fit us for eternity is one of serene detachment. The life of Jesus is a living reminder of the inevitability of struggle and conflict on the part of those who would be disciples. Yet somehow we have to learn the daily discipline of seeing all we do in the context of eternity—'*sub specie aeternitatis*' as the church Fathers of old liked to say. The poet T. S. Eliot expresses the same truth more lyrically:

> Teach us to care and not to care
> Teach us to be still
> Even among these rocks
> Our peace in His will.[29]

However we view the prospect of heaven, whether in terms of creative endeavour or endless delight (and the two are not mutually exclusive we should remember) we can be sure of one thing: heaven is God's gift to his people. The prayer of General Thanksgiving[30] acknowledges this when it says: 'We bless you for our creation, preservation and all the blessings of this life.' Creation and preservation alike testify to the belief that the God who loves us now will not abandon us when our earthly journey is over. God would be a travesty of everything which Christianity affirms him to be[31] if he endowed us with immortal longings and then snuffed us out like a spent candle at the end of our lives. 'Thou hast made us unto thyself,' said St Augustine, 'and our hearts are restless until they find their rest in thee.' The longing of the human heart presumes its fulfilment just as hunger presupposes the existence of bread.

In all of this we may be mistaken of course. It may ultimately prove to be the case that within the providence of God the destiny of all living things is extinction and nothing more. But in that event Christianity would surely not be wrong in interpreting such a fate as a sign of divine indifference wholly at odds with the unconditional love of God declared in the cross of Christ.[32]

Because heaven is God's gift we are right to view it as 'a sure and certain hope'.[33] To believe in the life of the world to come is (properly understood) to say nothing more than we believe in God. Heaven is God's business, not ours. Our hope rests in him and not in ourselves—in, for example, the belief that without God we may still enter paradise because we are by nature indestructible.

This notion owes much more to the doctrine of the immortality of the soul first postulated by the Greek philosopher Socrates (469–399 BC) than anything to be found in the New Testament—particularly in the writings of St Paul on the resurrection of the dead.[34] To be human is to suffer and in the end to die. We are, at the last, food for the earth or fuel for the fire. 'Earth to earth, ashes to ashes, dust to dust'—the Prayer Book does not equivocate concerning the awesome finality of death.

All the more amazing, then, is the assertion that 'as in Adam all die, even so in Christ shall all be made alive'.[35] The late evening service of Compline has a marvellous prayer which begins: 'Lord Jesus Christ, Son of the living God who at this evening hour didst rest in the sepulchre and didst thereby sanctify the grave to be a bed of hope to thy people . . .' Nowhere else in Scripture is the sheer audacity of the Christian message expressed so pointedly: hope is born in the grave that would hold us fast. This is God's work: the initiative comes from the One who raised Jesus Christ from the dead, 'and gave us new birth into a living hope and an inheritance that nothing can destroy . . .'[36]

Heaven is God's gift. To believe this is still to take seriously the complex issues that arise from the assumption that we as individuals will continue to be held in existence by the divine will after death. What do we mean by saying that somebody dies on earth and lives on in heaven? What departs from here and arrives there? What sort of physics might be required for people to be in touch with one another there, and how shall we recognize each other? These are serious questions requiring considerably more space and scrutiny than is available here.[37] Whatever answers we arrive at we may be sure (as science continues to demonstrate with disarming frequency) that the universe is more complex than current understanding assumes to be the case. In short, a doctrine of resurrection is not a fatuous claim, but may in the end prove to be a faithful reflection of hitherto unimaginable facts.

We have said nothing of hell and judgement. Down the centuries many lives have been blighted by the fear of 'the wrath to come'. Human imagination has seized too readily upon the prospect of impending tortures for the wicked, and has in the process lost sight of the divine love portrayed in the Gospels going to every length to seek and save those who are lost. Judgement we can live with—our moral sense leaves us in no doubt that all our actions, for good or ill, have consequences. But the idea that God requires or even enjoys the endless torment of sinners is so morally odious as to constitute 'a real blot on the Christian faith'.[38] We are not free to write off hell as a distortion of the gospel—the New Testament makes no provision for such licence. But we are right to suppose that mercy and forgiveness have the last word if the good news of Jesus Christ is to make any sense at all.

We draw this chapter to a close by returning briefly to the scene where we began: the garden of remembrance and the inscription on the plaque 'SAFE IN THE ARMS OF JESUS'. How can we know? How can we be completely sure that it's all true—that in the end we shall be safe? To ask such questions is to ask too much—'Ah what a dusty answer gets the soul when hot for certainties in this life.'[39] It's not that the questions are improper—we are by nature after all insatiably curious—but it is the nature of the case that no evidence exists that would still our deepest fears. We need instead to rely on our experience of this life to find firm ground concerning what happens when we die.

What Jesus said about 'taking no thought for the morrow' is particularly significant when we contemplate a future beyond the grave. The truly important thing is to recognize that even now when we seem frequently to be overwhelmed by hurts (real or imagined), we can, incredibly, find renewed strength and the glimmer of fresh possibilities. Hope repeatedly proves more contagious than despair. We can choose to face death with confidence because we have already experienced a fore-taste of the life we call eternal, and it is bound up with our sense of the steadfastness of God—the rock on which our hope is founded. Resurrection on this view becomes more than a pious hope or a comforting doctrine. It is felt, as the poet Keats puts it, 'on the pulse'—as a truth to sustain us both in life and death; a truth born out of trust that 'safe shall be my going, secretly armed against all death's endeavour; safe though all safety's lost; safe where men fall.'[40]

When we have come to this point of view and allowed it to shape our lives we shall find ourselves in the company of all those who have gone before us carrying in their hearts those sublime words of St Paul as he made his own pilgrimage to the new Jerusalem:

What then shall we say to this? If God is for us, who is against us? . . . And who shall separate us from the love of Christ? Shall tribulation, or distress, or persecution, or fam-ine, or nakedness, or peril, or sword? . . . No, in all these things we are more than conquerors through him who loved us. For I am sure that neither death nor life, nor angels, nor principalities, nor things present, nor things to come, nor powers, nor height nor depth, nor anything else in all creation will be able to separate us from the love of God in Christ Jesus our Lord.[41]

FOR REFLECTION

The message of the day is simple: the enduring human problem is how to cope with loss, sorrow and death; how to live through the endless endingness of everything. All that going down into the grave, all those leaves falling and grasses withering, and every year's death; and all those crosses on bare hillsides. How do we explain it, endure it? In a world like ours where death is seen as the final deprivation it is no wonder that we mourn our own mortality. What sorrow we must feel as we contemplate life for it is always slipping away.

It has always been thus and yet we know that our fore-fathers in the faith lived in the strong light of eternity. For them the things that are seen were passing and must never be strongly depended on: while the things that are unseen were eternal, real and lasting.

The legacy of their faith is not all we have. We have the hope of eternal life. We have our Lord's strong courage in the face of death and the certainty of life beyond it. We have the witness of the saints of the ages who were not burdened with the sorrow of time's passing. And we have the days when if we listen and hold ourselves still we can feel the saints and all our own dear dead beside us. They too join with angels and archangels and all the company of heaven, praising the God who contains all our yesterdays and in whom all loss and sorrow are healed.

(Bishop Richard Holloway)

O Lord Jesus Christ, Son of the living God, who at this evening hour didst rest in the sepulchre, and didst thereby

HEAVEN

sanctify the grave to be a bed of hope to thy people; make us so to abound in sorrow for our sins, which were the cause of thy Passion, that when our bodies lie in the dust our souls may live with thee, who livest and reignest with the Father and the Holy Ghost, ever one God, world without end. Amen

(Sarum Encheiridion)
(Compline Prayer)

We shall rest and we shall see; we shall see, and we shall love; we shall love, and we shall praise. Behold what shall be, in the end, and shall not end.

(Augustine—*City of God* XXII 30)

Then I saw a new heaven and a new earth; for the first heaven and the first earth had passed away, and the sea was no more. And I saw the holy city, new Jerusalem, coming down out of heaven from God, prepared as a bride adorned for her husband; and I heard a loud voice from the throne saying, 'Behold, the dwelling of God is with men. He will dwell with them, and they shall be his people, and God himself will be with them; he will wipe away every tear from their eyes, and death shall be no more, neither shall there be mourning nor crying nor pain any more, for the former things have passed away.'

And he who sat upon the throne said, 'Behold, I make all things new.' Also he said, 'Write this, for these words are trustworthy and true.' And he said to me, 'It is done! I am the Alpha and the Omega, the beginning and the end. To the thirsty I will give from the fountain of the water of life without payment. He who conquers shall have this heritage, and I will be his God and he shall be my son.'

(Rev. 21.1–7)

Blessed art thou, O Lord King of the universe, who dost make sleep to fall upon our eyes. Suffer us, O Lord God, to lie down in peace and to rise again therein. Let not ill thoughts trouble us, nor evil dreams and fantasies, but let our rest be perfect before thee. Lighten our eyes that we sleep not in death. Blessed be thou, O Lord, who in thy glory dost give light to all the world. Amen

(Jewish)

We give thanks to thee, O Lord, who hast preserved us through the day; and to thee we pay our vows for protection through the coming night; bring us in safety to the morning hours, we beseech thee, that so thou mayest at all times receive our praise. Through Christ our Lord. Amen

(Gelasian Sacramentary)

O Lord God, who art light eternal, in the brightness of whose countenance is day that knows no night, and in whose protecting arms all quietness and tranquillity: while the darkness covers the face of the earth, receive our body and soul unto thy care and keeping; that whether we sleep or wake we may rest in thee, in thy light beholding light. Through Jesus Christ our Lord. Amen

(Jeremy Taylor)

FIVE

*

A Proper Life:
Being Human Now

IN ONE OF his books Martin Buber relates a story first told by Rabbi Hanokh concerning a rather stupid man. Each morning as he got out of bed he had difficulty in remembering where he had left his clothes the night before. This became such a problem that he dreaded going to sleep. He dealt with the dilemma by taking a pencil and paper with him to his bedroom. As he undressed he jotted down where he placed everything. The next morning he looked at the paper. It said, 'trousers—on chair', so he put them on; 'shoes—under bed', so he put them on; he carried on in this fashion until he was fully dressed. Then he said to himself: 'Now, where am I?' He checked the list on his paper but there was no answer. 'And that', said the rabbi, 'is how it is with man.'[1]

Jewish wisdom speaks to many of us in this pithy tale, for quite often we don't know where we are. We come into the world without a compass; we are easily confused concerning our destiny as human beings, and the one certainty is that we shall die. But before then (and in full acceptance of our mortality) we have to live—live as much as we can, using the time life has placed at our disposal along with the gifts and abilities that are uniquely ours. We have the freedom to neglect or develop these rather like the servants in the Gospel parable of the talents,[2] and on our better days we shall be mindful that the hours and opportunities alike are given on trust from God. Words like 'care' and 'responsibility' come naturally to mind once we recognize that a little bit of the world's history has been entrusted to us. Our existence is a gift, and we can best show our gratitude by treating with reverence and respect all that we have and own.

Before our concern for stewardship moves us to save the rain forests we have to save ourselves. Rabbis do not tell artful tales merely to entertain; they ask to be heeded. The question relating to where we are as human beings is pertinent because it hardly makes sense to begin any undertaking—especially the huge business of becoming a person—without knowledge of the resources available to us and the impedimenta that might obstruct our progress. A modest inquiry into our humanity is called for if only to save us from inflicting needless damage on ourselves or others.

Our consideration of prayer has already given us some essential data. We know that we are ragged inside—neither demon nor angel but certainly wracked with ambiguities. Each possibility we possess is accompanied by its opposite, so the hand which paints the Sistine Chapel can also consign innocents to the ovens of Auschwitz. We are shot through with contradictions, as the sardonic lines of the poet Alexander Pope make clear:

> Created half to rise and half to fall;
> Great lord of all things, yet a prey to all;
> Sole judge of truth in endless error hurled:
> The glory, jest and riddle of the world![3]

It feels uncomfortable being a conundrum, and perplexity can easily arise if we gaze too long in the mirror. We see a riddle that might in part be resolved by the discipline of prayer. But what else is presented to us? Without being too self-congratulatory (given our capacity for atrocious cruelties) we should wish to say that, despite all our affinities with the higher animals and the fact that we are descended from animal ancestors, we are of a different order. We can stand on our feet, compose love sonnets, transform the sexual act into something mystical, and contemplate our deaths. We are hounded by the claim of conscience, and know ourselves to be more than just a bundle of appetites. There is our marked thirst for knowledge and our awareness of transience—that we are caught inextricably in the web of time. We are dust to the bone but:

> in that dust is wrought
> a place for visions, a hope
> that reaches beyond the stars,
> conjures and pauses the seas;
> dust discovers our own
> proud, torn destinies.[4]

How extraordinary that we can recognize ourselves as finite yet containing longings for new horizons and impossible dreams. This quest for 'something more' drives us on; not in terms of acquiring more clutter in our already congested lives but in the hope that deeper and more enriching truths are still to be discovered beyond the boundaries of our present experience. A remarkable feature of Brian Keenan's savage captivity in Lebanon was his quite incredible capacity to suffer pain and humiliation on a scale few of us will ever know, and still be able to evaluate his own responses to degradation and the motives of his mindless torturers. He was concerned to concentrate not on what was done to him, but on what he could make of what was done to him. As a consequence, understanding rather than bitterness was the strange fruit of his season in hell.

This is transcendence of a different sort which set alongside the other redeeming features of our lives should stop us from accepting uncritically any account of human nature that reduces us to nothing more than an accident of evolution or a mere collocation of atoms. We are ambiguous rather than absurd, and the way we answer the question: 'Are we glory, jest or riddle?' will affect the way we live and what we become.

At the very least we can say that the apparent contradictions within us do not imply that we are a mishap or an unfortunate jest. In fact these tensions and polarities may provide the only conditions that make possible distinctively human lives. Rats after all, as far as we know, show no particular enthusiasm for moral issues and questions of meaning; and chimpanzees, delightful though they are, are not normally to be seen on our streets collecting money for impoverished chimpanzees they will never meet.

In our struggle to discover where we are and what might lie before us we can find help in an early Christian understanding of what our humanity entails. Although many centuries old, the insights to be derived from thinkers like Irenaeus[5] anticipated modern views of the person as a self-transcendent being. The Greek Fathers[6] in particular saw human life as a progression—as a response to God's gracious calling of humanity to communion with himself. There was the ever-present likelihood on our part of slipping back and failing, but always there was held out to us the possibility of finally coming to share in the 'likeness' of God.[7] Somewhat at variance with the fashionable pessimism of our own day, they did not shrink from describing the purpose of our earthly sojourning as the 'deification' of humanity. There could hardly be a more noble vocation, and intimations of it were to be found in the New Testament. The second letter of Peter spoke of our becoming 'partakers of the divine nature,'[8] and Paul testified that believers 'beholding the glory of the Lord were being changed into his likeness from one degree of glory to another'.[9]

This ancient teaching is important. It reflects the height and depth of the human condition—our unsatisfied longings and desires, and the morass of our inner lives that frequently stymies our development as persons. More significantly, it enables us to believe in ourselves as individuals who in spite of a 'natural proclivity to sinfulness'[10] are nevertheless capable of greatness and goodness. The riddle confronts us again: we can (and often do) spend too much of our time 'licking the earth',[11] but we also have the potential to become God-like and share in the divine life. This realism is bracing and heartening: a 'proper life' is an attainable ideal, not some whimsical product of the imagination. We can actually love, learn, suffer, and create in ways that make the word 'humanity' constitute a sublime utterance.

The perfect embodiment of this ideal can be seen in the life of Jesus of Nazareth. His openness to his own destiny, his obedience to God, and his obvious passion for life and people led Luther to describe him as 'the proper man'.[12] The New Testament gives us only the outlines of his life yet, unmistakably, a personality emerges that captivates and then controls those who will bear his teaching. Millions have fallen prey to his spell, and language has laboured to contain his meaning. Alexander Cruden, compiling his concordance to the Bible in the eighteenth century, listed two hundred names and images which have been applied to him.

Why all this veneration should be accorded to one person is a perennial question beyond our scope here, but it does challenge us to consider what in the end is so compelling and decisive about an itinerant teacher with no academic pretensions and absolutely nothing by way of worldly prestige. Why this man? His abiding significance must stem crucially from the events of Easter. Dead men do not normally rise from the grave, and without the message of the resurrection the gospel could not have been presented as good news. Consequently, as one new Testament scholar has expresseed it, there would have been 'no faith, no Church, no worship, no prayer in Christendom to this day'[13] without the original conviction that the tomb was empty and the occupant free.

If the resurrection vindicates the life and teaching of Jesus, it does not of itself fully explain why he continues to speak so powerfully to our condition. The answer must lie in the quality of his life. He was not just 'the man for others'; he also brought a shining integrity to his own goals and vocation. He responded gladly to the demands people made upon him, but his response was ordered by his own central commitments. Above all else he was concerned to offer his listeners a new vision of the world as a place where they could reach their perfection not through what they had or did but entirely through what they were. He told his friends to be themselves and not to be always worrying about other things. Instead of striving for security and power and always seeing others as potential threats, followers were summoned to love their neighbours, have compassion, and hold fast to God. Belief in the reality, love, and power of God led to a way of life that was built upon enduring foundations, while to live in the opposite way was to go against the grain of things and ultimately court disaster. The parable of the two houses built on sand and on rock made it all very plain.[14]

Others may have said similar things but unlike them Jesus taught with the authority of one who embodied his teaching—who, indeed, practised what he preached and was consequently at home in the world, free to enjoy its pleasures, and ready, when the time came, to suffer its rejection. Again, others have suffered the obloquy of public derision, and many have died humiliating deaths. But there is, nevertheless, something awesome about the cross of Golgotha: if it reveals God's costly identification with human sin and suffering it also exposes our readiness to crucify divine love rather than be conformed to its demands. The anguish of Jesus and the awful ambivalence precipitated in people's lives by his message evoke the deepest pathos:

> I am not moved to love thee, my Lord God
> by heaven thou hast promised me:
> I am not moved by the sore dreaded hell
> to forebear me from offending thee
>
> I am moved by thee Lord: I am moved
> at seeing thee nailed upon the cross and mocked:
> I am moved by thy body all over wounds:
> I am moved by thy dishonour and thy death
>
> I am moved, last, by thy love, in such a wise that though
> there were no heaven I still should love thee,
> and though there were no hell I still should fear thee.

I need no gift of thee to make me love thee,
For though my present hope were all despair,
as now I love thee I should love thee still.[15]

The Passion of Christ looms so large in our consciousness that
it is tempting to construe the Gospels as little more than a four-
part presentation of the 'man of sorrows acquainted with
grief'.[16] This is a mistake, albeit an understandable one, that in
history has led to much needless misery on the part of those
who have come to identify discipleship exclusively in terms of
self-denial. The presumption appears to be that only by imitat-
ing Jesus in his suffering and abandonment can we hope to
embrace the Christian ideal.

In George Eliot's novel, *The Mill on the Floss*, her impulsive
heroine Maggie Tulliver acquires a copy of the *Imitation of
Christ* by Thomas à Kempis. His warnings about 'enjoying our
own will and pleasure' are heeded and then she comes to a
passage which exhorts her to 'pluck up and destroy that hidden
inclination to thyself, and unto all private and earthly good . . .
Forsake thyself, resign thyself.' From then on she refuses to
look at herself in the mirror, lies on the floor at night, denies
herself the music and books which she loves (except the
church organ and sacred literature), and then informs the
young man who loves her: 'I wish we could have been
friends . . . But that is the trial I have to bear in everything . . .
I must part with everything I cared for when I was a child. And
I must part with you.'[17]

This is hardly a proper life—in fact it spawns the kind of
religion that critics have rightly condemned as life-denying,
selfish, and wholly lacking in charity. We have to take up our
cross and follow Jesus, but discipleship also invites to do much
else. We are to consider the lilies of the field for example, and
to love little children; to enjoy food and wine and the conviv-
iality of table talk; to see the good earth as a source of endless
delight; and to rejoice in the fact that we are 'fearfully and
wonderfully made'.[18] Is it so strange after all to think of Jesus

laughing and joking in the presence of friends? To see him telling fantastic stories in order to make a point? To imagine him holding Mary spellbound at his feet by his sheer vivacity as Martha scuttled about organizing the food? Jesus was more than an agonized and broken figure on a gibbet; he comes to us as an attractive man—young, curious, energetic for the mission, and willing others to share in the venture. None of this detracts from the meaning of his Passion or the sombre side of his teaching. But it does challenge us to see Jesus in all his humanity and to live with the same sort of abandon.

Perhaps celebration is the word we are looking for: a celebration of the joys of life and ourselves, as a proper expression of our gratitude to God and our pleasure in being alive. Centuries ago the rabbis used to remind their congregations that a person would have 'to give an account on the Judgement Day of every good thing which he might have enjoyed and did not'. Given the poverty and persecution that marked Jewish life through succeeding generations this might seem on first glance a rather cavalier remark. But the rabbis knew their Scriptures emphasized the goodness of creation. Tragedy and scepticism could be found in Lamentations, Job, and Ecclesiastes but joy and delight in equal measure characterized other writings.

With our impoverished understanding of the Old Testament today it is almost impossible to understand how Jewish life endured so much desolation unless we come to realize how enlivening the knowledge of the Bible was for reader and listener. Few could be scholars and know the books by heart, but everyone could imbibe their spirit through the feasts and fasts of the Jewish year. There were psalms to recite on all kinds of celebratory occasions—most obviously the great 150th psalm with its invitation to 'everything that has breath' to 'praise the Lord!' There was the Song of Songs with its love poetry setting down in exquisite form the pleasure that one person could find in another. The book of Proverbs pointed to the happiness to be found in family life, with Chapter 31 in particular praising the mother as the architect of domestic contentment: 'A woman of worth who can find her? For her price is above rubies. The heart of her husband trusteth in her . . . her children rise up and call her blessed.' The prophets through their utterances spoke to the people with a passionate intensity, and characters like Saul and David, Deborah, Samson, and Delilah seized their imagination. It cannot be said too often that Jesus was a Jew; that he would have been familiar with everything we have just noted, for he went to the synagogue 'as was his custom'[19] and belonged to a human family replete with brothers and sisters.[20] Like the prophets before him he would have seen that the whole earth was filled with the glory of God, and that each day was a day made by the Lord of creation. Everyday life therefore (and not just the special sphere designated spiritual) had to take on a religious meaning, and be lived and celebrated in relation to God.

This kind of faith embodies the sanctification of all things, views creation itself as a sacramental sign of God's goodness—every person sacred, every living thing holy—and, by implication, extols the glories of art and science, of music and literature, of love and pleasure as our birthright. We are to enjoy the world, and through its miraculous loveliness come to a deeper awareness and praise of God himself. The blind and rigid asceticism embraced by Maggie Tulliver seems not to understand or care for any of this; she is destined to 'desire communion with none'; 'remove herself far away from acquaintance and dear friends'; 'attend wholly unto God and herself and keep her mind void of all temporal comfort'.[21]

Sadly, there is nothing idiosyncratic here that would enable us to dismiss such extreme renunciation as a caricature of a religious approach to life. Christianity has never lacked its baleful influences; certain teachings of the early centuries in particular elevated celibacy, continence, and virginity as the highest human aspirations.[22] The human body was no longer to be regarded as part of the natural order, and the vulnerability of the flesh to delight and temptation called for the severest discipline. The libido had to be kept in check and the pleasures of the world renounced. By the fifth century, monasteries and convents had emerged, and wives began to disappear from the homes of the clergy. The cult of the Virgin Mary came into flower, and a small but influential élite walked the streets of every city within the Roman Empire. Celibate priests and nuns enjoined long periods of fasting and the avoidance of wine and mixed company. The intimacy of marriage far from affording delight and tenderness became tainted with guilt and shame, and couples unable to embrace celibacy were encouraged to perform the act of intercourse as quickly and as uninterestingly as possible.[23]

This was an oppressive legacy to bequeath to later ages. While we should not wish to condemn teachings and practices that seem to us now pointless or bizarre, it is a matter of regret that a distorted view of human sexuality informed the attitude of the Church to the body. Increasingly, the human person came to be seen as an unfinished block requiring 'the deep chisel bites of renunciation if the Christian was to take on the lineaments of the risen Christ'.[24] In our concern today for a way of life that is not chilled by the melancholy of an exaggerated asceticism, our capacity for enjoyment should not be confused with self-indulgence or the desire to possess things. In a different way this can prove just as disastrous a course of action as sterile renunciation. Our possessions have a habit of swallowing us up: the satisfaction of one desire quickly generates another and we can easily be dragged along by impulses beyond our control. St Augustine was alert to this tendency fifteen centuries ago, and he describes what moral theologians have called 'concupiscence' in the following terms:

If you love to possess things, then you will desire the whole earth so that all who are born in it shall be your vassals and slaves. And when the whole of the earth is yours what then? You will ask for the sea in which you cannot live. The fish shall outdo you in this kind of greed. But perhaps the islands may be yours. Do not rest content with them, ask for the air. . . . let your desire reach even to the stars; say that the sun is yours . . .[25]

The more possessions we have the more anxiety they generate. We are burdened by the need to protect them from predators; in extreme cases (usually experienced by the very affluent) precious objects have to be locked away in vaults and brought out occasionally like holy relics to be venerated. This would have amused Augustine, for he had come to see in his middle years (and not least from reflecting on the rapacious desires of his own youth) that in the end we can possess nothing. In fact we are wise to practise the art of losing—of sitting lightly to the things we own and not worrying overmuch if we have to forfeit them. We can enjoy their beauty or utility without being dominated by them.

This calls for a healthy asceticism which responds readily and gladly to the world's intoxicating beauty, but places a question mark against acquisitiveness. The earliest account of a Christian community records that: 'Everything was held in common . . . all who had property sold it and brought the proceeds to the apostles who distributed it to any who stood in need.'[26] The resonances of this passage should not be lost on us. In its unpretentious way it stands as a 'sign of contradiction' against conspicuous consumption, and challenges us to see the earth as a common treasury for the delight and relief of all. More than any generation before we are acutely aware of the pernicious effect of poverty among communities everywhere. Our approach to material things will reflect this but not, we must add, by a dubious refusal to enjoy ourselves so long as human misery persists. There is nothing incongruous or immoral in our enjoyment of life even in the knowledge that many have no access to the banquet. Of course, we must remember the poor, but our humanity will be a curmudgeonly thing if all we can do is wring our hands at the horrors of existence as pleasures pass us by.

Modern theology is much more open to the legitimacy of pleasure—particularly in the hitherto taboo area of sexual relationships. Marriage is now seen as a gift of God in creation so that: 'With delight and tenderness husband and wife may know each other in love and through the joy of their bodily union may strengthen the union of their heart and lives.'[27] Delight, tenderness, and joy; these are lovely words conveying the liberating truths that sexual desire is not unseemly, that the body is not a thing of shame, that lovemaking is not simply about producing children but awakening us to the unimaginably wonderful dimensions of deep sexual experience.

Imagination, creativity, playfulness; uncomplicated longings and the most tender affections are all integral to the act of becoming one flesh. And in the giving of ourselves to another in this most intimate of ways we may come to learn something of that transforming love which 'delights in the truth and is never selfish'.[28] This is an ideal, of course, and one which we know from experience can easily be distorted or devalued. Love can become possessive, and deny freedom and individuality to the beloved. And not infrequently two people may be so closely intertwined that they are never able to see beyond their immediate preoccupation with each other. Love is debased as soon as it is confined in this way, and becomes little more than a veiled form of self-regard.

A wholesome asceticism is required in our personal relationships no less than in our attitude to possessions. We are not to insist on our own way, and there will be times when delight is freely set aside because of other claims. Sexual love is precious but should not be so prized that it blinds us to the truth: like possessions it has enormous power to enhance our lives; and like the material things we cherish most we need to be free to forego it—either voluntarily or out of simple necessity should circumstances require. We are sexual beings, but we are also persons who value each other independently of the joy afforded by physical union. Sexual fulfilment is not the only paradigm we possess; celibacy will be the radiant way for some and, for others, mutual support and comfort will matter more than fleeting joy. Lovers are also companions and friends. Our basic need here as persons is to secure what St Augustine called 'the right ordering of our loving'—putting our desires and affections in proper order for the sake of our integration and wholeness.

We have to be decision-makers. Either by accepting or rejecting the various possibilities presented to us (and not just in the sphere of an intimate relationship) we are determining the direction of our lives and those of others. We are shaped by our choices; to decide on one course of action is to forfeit another. The root meaning of the word 'decision' is 'cutting off'. Important decisions always carry implications, and much needless hurt can be avoided when as a matter of principle, we have an eye for the long view in human affairs.

Deliberation over human issues is always a costly business but it does disclose in a quite vivid way the sense of freedom we feel as persons. Freedom is a notoriously elusive concept, but this has never stopped men and women praying for it and sometimes dying for it. Even when due acknowledgement is made of the various factors which limit us—temperament, intelligence, education, social status, the time and place in which we find ourselves—we still presuppose freedom in our thoughts and actions. Bishop Butler, in *The Analogy of Religion*, puts this very neatly when he points out that since we all act on the assumption of freedom it is far simpler to grant that it does, as a matter of fact, really exist.[29]

A paradox that we may be reluctant to note here is how quickly we can shrink back from the freedom we profess to crave once it is offered to us. The heel of someone's boot on our face is, to be sure, oppressive, but once it is removed and light floods in, are we ready to embrace the attendant anxiety of a wholly new situation filled in equal measure with threat and promise? As an observable fact far too many of us opt for security and mediocrity; safety is preferred to the spirit of adventure, and the open road is made the prerogative of the young.

To deny that we are free to choose or to reject the opportunities freedom brings in its train is to suffer the slow haemorrhaging of our humanity. Without our freedom as individuals and the belief that we contain the potential of as yet undiscovered life, we may as well be a teapot or a lawnmower or a cuddly toy. But we are none of these things: we are instead 'God's work of art'[30]—partners with him in the continuing work of creation.

To live creatively should not be understood in the narrow sense. We are not all required to hew form out of marble or through the struggle of brain and pen arrange words in such a way that the reader will be consoled or challenged. Our task is more direct: out of the stuff of our lives can we fashion something that is worthy and true? Can we embrace the freedom offered to us and commit ourselves to strenuous ideals? And in case this all seems rather earnest and imposing can we also laugh and play, take time to smell the roses, and through 'the senses five' see the divine glory radiating all things? The mystics and poets have laboured long to tell us that we live in a transfigured world where the familiar scenes of earth are shot through with the eternal reality of heaven. It is all a matter of seeing. Here is the seventeenth-century poet Thomas Traherne inviting us to look with fresh eyes at our world:

> You will never enjoy the world aright, till you are clothed with the heavens and crowned with the stars . . . till your spirit filleth the whole world and the stars are your jewels; till you are familiar with the way of God in all ages as with your walk and table . . . till you delight in God for being good to all: you never enjoy the world.[31]

These words take me back to Israel—to Jerusalem and a pilgrimage I made there with others in the autumn of 1993. I had been several times before but on this occasion decided to take my group to the Holocaust Museum. We were there for the better part of an afternoon, making our way in silence through the labyrinth of rooms that contained all we needed to know (and could probably bear to know) about the systematic decimation of a proud and cultured people. The conversation was subdued on the coach as we made our way back to the hotel. The following morning we went to the Western Wall. The scene was familiar to me but no less compelling: the faithful at prayer; police maintaining a discreet presence in the background; a brilliant blue sky overhead; and everywhere the swirl of activity and movement. It felt a good place to be in—a strong sense of coming home. We moved among the crowds with ease and enjoyment. As we approached the wall, activity suddenly intensified. There was music, singing, and dancing; splashes of vivid colour everywhere; excited voices; and laughter—prodigious, unrestrained, spontaneous laughter. Boys could be seen astride their fathers' shoulders; mothers and sisters were throwing what looked like confetti. The moment celebrations seemed to be petering out another voice would burst forth in song, and the laughter and music would begin all over again. By sheer good fortune we had come to the bar mitzvah parties—the joyful aftermath of a ceremony where Jewish boys reach their majority and begin the crucial transition from child to man.

For me personally this was much more than a party. I had witnessed, quite unexpectedly, the triumph of life over death, of love over evil, of celebration over despair. We were no more than a few miles from the Holocaust Museum and the memories of the previous day were vivid. But here there was only affirmation of life, praise of God, joy in being human. It was as if a pageant had been arranged to convey the scriptural truth that 'many waters cannot quench love, neither can floods drown it.'[32] Much later the words of the poet Dylan Thomas came back to me: 'And death shall have no dominion.'[33]

I had to go to Israel to learn this old truth. I should have remembered the Hasidic story of a poor rabbi in Cracow who dreamed that there was a great treasure buried under the bridge in front of the royal palace in Prague. He set out for the city to see if he could gain this treasure. On arrival he found that the bridge was carefully guarded. After some days of loitering and speculating he was drawn into conversation with one of the guards and found himself disclosing that he had dreamed that there was treasure there. 'Why', the guard exclaimed, 'you are a fool! Only last night I dreamed about a rabbi in Cracow, looking very much like you, who had treasure buried in his backyard. But you don't think I'd be fool enough to set off for Cracow in search of it.'[34]

We have treasure in the backyard. But often we shall not find it unless we are prepared to go on a long journey and learn about it from a stranger. Israel opened my eyes again to the place of celebration in human life—to the fact that we celebrate too little and are generally more conscious of the shadows and the dark than the light which is not overcome by them.[35]

Part of our difficulty is that we are often too absorbed with life in a wrong sense—so concerned to impose our own agenda on each new day that we miss the 'many splendoured thing'. The old city of Jerusalem is filled with street traders who allow life to address them. They make their modest deals often sitting patiently for hours, and life passes. In a curious way they are open to its possibilities in a way that we are not. They smile; they have time to notice things—the minutiae in this strange, familiar, yet mysterious continuum we call the present. Life is made up of small, precious details, but we feel we have to simplify, and in our busy lives it hardly pays to bother about apparent trifles.

In the streets of India at filthy street corners, images of gods can be found with garlands of fresh flowers about their necks. Divinity can be gleaned at every turn for those with eyes to see. On the road between illusion and reality there are all kinds of clues and signals—places to pause, faces to gaze on, minute particulars to be observed containing within them a whole world of meaning.[36] But beauty and truth will always go on their way unapprehended unless we bring a particular energy, discipline even, to our way of looking. We need a lively eye and the humility to recognize that there is still everything to learn.

A PROPER LIFE

When the rich learned Pharisee
Came to consult him secretly
Upon his heart with iron pen
He wrote, 'Ye must be born again.'[37]

FOR REFLECTION

From Dear Theo: An Autobiography of Vincent Van Gogh from His Letters, *edited by* Irving Stone

Oh, my dear Theo, if you could see the olive groves just now! The leaves like old silver, and silver turning to green against the blue, and the orange-coloured ploughed earth. It is something quite different from your idea of it in the North. It is like the pollard willows of our Dutch meadows or the oak bushes of our dunes; the rustle of an olive grove has something very secret in it, and immensely old. It is too beautiful for us to dare to paint it or to be able to imagine it.

The figure of a labourer—some furrows in a ploughed field—a bit of sand, sea and sky—are serious subjects, so difficult, but at the same time so beautiful, that it is indeed worth while to devote one's life to the task of expressing the poetry hidden in them.

From Gitanjali *by* Rabindranath Tagore

LVII

Light, my light, the world-filling light, the eye-kissing light, heart-sweetening light!

Ah; the light dances, my darling, at the centre of my life; the light strikes, my darling, the chords of my love; the sky opens, the wind runs wild, laughter passes over the earth.

The butterflies spread their sails on the sea of light. Lilies and jasmines surge up on the crest of the waves of light.

A PROPER LIFE

The light is shattered into gold on every cloud, my darling, and it scatters gems in profusion.

Mirth spreads from leaf to leaf, my darling, and gladness without measure. The heaven's river has drowned its banks and the flood of joy is abroad.

From The Collected Poems of Stevie Smith

NOT WAVING BUT DROWNING

Nobody heard him, the dead man,
But still he lay moaning:
I was much further out than you thought
And not waving but drowning.

Poor chap, he always loved larking
And now he's dead
It must have been too cold for him his heart gave way,
They said.

Oh, no no no, it was too cold always
(Still the dead one lay moaning)
I was much too far out all my life
And not waving but drowning.

From The Collected Poems of George Herbert

THE FLOWER

How fresh, O Lord, how sweet and clean
Are thy returns! ev'n as the flowers in spring;
To which, besides their own demean,
The late-past frosts tributes of pleasure bring.
Grief melts away
Like snow in May,
As if there were no such cold thing.

THE BIG QUESTIONS

        Who could have thought my shrivel'd heart
Could have recover'd greennesse? It was gone
        Quite underground; as flowers depart
To see their mother-root, when they have blown;
           Where they together
           All the hard weather,
Dead to the world, keep house unknown.

        And now in age I bud again,
After so many deaths I live and write;
        I once more smell the dew and rain,
And relish versing: O my onely light,
           It cannot be
           That I am he
On whom thy tempest fell all night.

        These are thy wonders, Lord of love,
To make us see we are but flowers that glide:
        Which when we once can finde and prove,
Thou hast a garden for us, where to bide.
           Who would be more,
           Swelling through store,
Forfeit their Paradise by their pride.

A PROPER LIFE

God our creator,
you have made us one with this earth,
to tend it and to bring forth fruit;
may we so respect and cherish
all that has life from you,
that we may share in the labour of all creation
to give birth to your hidden glory,
through Jesus Christ, Amen.

Christ, whose insistent call
disturbs our settled lives,
give us discernment to hear your word,
grace to relinquish our tasks,
and courage to follow emptyhanded
wherever you may lead;
that the voice of your gospel
may reach to the ends of the earth,
Amen.

O God who took human flesh
that you might be intimate with us;
may we so taste and touch you
in our bodily life
that we may discern and celebrate
your body in the world,
through Jesus Christ, Amen.

THE BIG QUESTIONS

Prayer For Grace

My hands will I lift up
unto Thy commandments which I have loved.
Open Thou mine eyes that I may see,
incline my heart that I may desire,
order my steps that I may follow,
  the way of Thy commandments.
O Lord God, be Thou to me a God,
  and beside Thee none else,
none else, nought else with Thee.

(Lancelot Andrewes)

O God, who hast taught us that all our doings without love are nothing worth; send down thy Holy Spirit, and pour into our hearts that most excellent gift of love, the very bond of peace and all virtues, without which whosoever liveth is counted dead before thee; Grant this for thine only Son Jesus Christ's sake.

(The Book of Common Prayer)

SIX

*

All Times Are His Seasons: The Offering of Worship

SOME MIGHT THINK it a little odd that a consideration of worship has been left until the final chapter. Traditionally regarded as the heartbeat of any authentically religious life, it could be argued that worship should have been the first of our explorations. My own view, however, is that it is not possible to give an adequate account of what is happening when people worship until we have grappled honestly with the issues raised in this book. We are right to be suspicious when easy answers are given to deceptively simple questions and, frankly, it will not do to present such a complex (and fascinating) subject as worship as nothing more than a spiritual massage for disconsolate souls or an adjunct of the entertainment industry. A church quite nearby once had a notice outside proclaiming 'WE ENJOY OUR WORSHIP'. We can be pleased for that congregation, particularly when we have just emphasized the importance of celebration in human life. But enjoyment alone, or for that matter, the need for comfort and reassurance hardly constitutes a decent explanation of the place and purpose of worship in the life of the Church. As we delve a little more we may come to see worship as a reaching out on our part to God, and a sharing of his presence in our midst with those who represent the household of faith. The implications of this two-fold movement are immense, but before we go further some preliminary remarks to provide a backcloth for our inquiry.

About five million people attend church each Sunday (a statistic worth bearing in mind when cynics suggest that organized religion is all but finished). They listen to around forty thousand sermons and, variously, share in the Eucharist, 'hear' Mass or praise the Lord. Some congregations favour 'open' prayer, and increasing numbers seem at ease with relaxed, informal services. Those with a love of ritual are helped by the trappings of ceremonial, and a minority retain a preference for the early morning quietness of the 'eight o'clock' Communion. The common denominator uniting all these diverse activities is that all those involved would understand themselves to be engaged in a very specific endeavour: the worship of God.

Would they, I wonder, say more? Would they agree with me, for instance, that worship is a strange undertaking? When comparisons have been made with other rituals—whether social, civic, or national—we know that when we make the sign of the cross, get down on our knees or confess ourselves unworthy before receiving bread and wine, we are doing something that has no exact parallel in any other sphere of life. In fact, an unseen and uncommitted observer at a church service might well be mystified by the occasion. It is, after all, a trifle uncommon in other situations for people to drink from a common cup or listen dutifully (and repeatedly) to a message that may be unedifying or presume familiarity with people they may hardly know.

But all these curious events happen every week in our own churches. We come to the altar rail momentarily unaware of the significant differences that generally divide us. Class, colour, and personal credentials strangely melt away as we are fed by the bread of life. Sermons are endured that are sometimes even worse than popular caricature. And the handclasp of peace is shared with others even though we may not know their names. We could go on to talk about the sad rather than strange fact that worship persists even in churches that are eaten up with boredom. Most of us will have experience of lifeless congregations where habit rather than conviction or expectation has brought the people dolefully together. The sermon no longer connects, and the service has a leaden predictability; joy and hope have long fled. The show goes on, but to no obvious purpose—clergy and congregation wedded to a ritual that seems to have lost any reality.

None of this is peculiar to our own generation. We may recall the severe sentence passed upon the church at Laodicea in the book of Revelation: 'I know all your ways; you are neither hot nor cold. . . . but because you are lukewarm, neither hot nor cold, I will spit you out of my mouth.'[1] Mediocrity in church life has a long pedigree, it seems. St Augustine as a pastoral bishop loved the Church passionately yet, by his own admission he knew the members of his congregation to be 'average sensual people'.[2] Our love of God can soon grow cold, and nowhere is this reflected more painfully than in worship where lips ostensibly honour God but hearts can be far from him.[3] It is tempting but wrong to lay the blame entirely on the clergy. When the great eighteenth-century evangelical preacher George Whitefield commented acidly that: 'The reason why congregations have been so dead is that they have dead men preaching to them', he was stating a partial truth. Many Anglican clergy of his day had made an easy compromise with the spirit of the age, reducing religion to little more than ethics and social control—parson and squire together as arbiters and upholders of the local peace.[4] But then the eighteenth century was sick of war and bloodshed all incurred in the name of God or Christ, so we should not be too surprised that religious enthusiasm was treated with scepticism or even disdain.

Perhaps the deeper truth behind Whitefield's lament is that in every age the Church stands in need of reform; the temptation for congregations to become Laodicean in spirit is perennial. Whether through excessive worldliness, spiritual pride or simple indolence we can miss the mark—no longer aware that the point of worship is to discover the gracious purposes of a living God. We step inside hallowed walls to be challenged as well as comforted; to respond with gratitude to the love of God; and to be drawn ever more deeply into the mystery of divine beauty and goodness. The Prayer for Purity of Heart at the beginning of the Anglican Communion Service concentrates the mind very well:

> Almighty God, to whom all hearts are open, all desires known, and from whom no secrets are hidden: cleanse the thoughts of our hearts by the inspiration of your Holy Spirit, that we may perfectly love you, and worthily magnify your holy name; through Christ our Lord. Amen.

The language is beautiful but the prayer is memorable chiefly for the way in which it sets down our priorities. We come into the presence of God, who knows the secrets of all our hearts. We are ragged inside, and we need to be cleansed. Worship 'disinfects us of our egoism'.[5] We long to taste and see how gracious the Lord is; through the ministry of word and sacrament and the fellowship of the congregation, the Spirit of God moves within us and deepens our love for Creator and creation alike. Worship is a duty on our part—a labour of love gladly undertaken, but always our response and effort are preceded by the initiative of God. So as we give thanks and confess and make our concerns known, we are not lobbying for favours in the courts of the Almighty. God goes before us, loves us before we love him, knows our needs before we ask, and like the father of the prodigal son seeks to bring us home even when we are far off.[6] Other examples could be given: when Isaiah entered the temple 'in the year that King Uzziah died' and received his call as a prophet, the Lord was already in that place 'seated high and exalted', surrounded by angelic creatures ceaselessly calling to one another: 'Holy, holy, holy is the Lord of hosts; the whole earth is full of his glory.'[7]

The Lord was already there; he did not have to be invoked. In the same way, when Jacob rested for the night on his way to Haran, he dreamt of a supernatural traffic between heaven and earth—'of a ladder with angels going up and down upon it'.[8]

When he awoke he acknowledged the awesome nature of his experience: 'Truly the Lord is in this place and I did not know it' and built an altar to represent the house of God. Jacob did not initiate the worship; what his dream had done was to disclose the meeting of heaven and earth that was already going on. In the dawn light he named the place Bethel (house of God) and made explicit what had before been unseen and unrecognized.

Worship is God's business; it is divine activity as well as 'the heart in pilgrimage'.[9] Unless both meanings are held together the worshipping life of a community is essentially no different than the various enthusiasms which bring like-minded people together—whether their passion is for bingo or bird-watching. Coming together, even for a common purpose, does not of itself constitute worship. Only when a community is caught up in something greater than the membership, that makes it feel of less importance, can we begin to talk of worship. The name traditionally given to this experience is the numinous,[10] the sacred and fascinating mystery experienced by Isaiah and Jacob and all those whose lives have been touched by God.

We could go on now to talk about the beauty of holiness and the ways in which we come to a sense of God as One who is, and lives, confessed by the world or not. Music and silence, preaching and prayer, and so much else can bring us to this heightened awareness, sometimes when we least expect it. We can be surprised by joy. The more important point, however, is not to see worship as a potent, ecstatic experience, and that anything less than this is somehow inferior or reflects badly on our own spiritual maturity. Ecstasy is not the sole end of worship, and we can be touched by God through the 'still small voice' heard by Elijah on the Mount of Horeb[11] or through a compelling word from lectern or pulpit that speaks exactly to our condition. Grace comes to us in many ways, and the need on our part is to be receptive to whatever might be disclosed. In this respect our understanding of the Church will affect our approach to worship. There is a difference between the view that regards a congregation as simply an assembly of people gathered for mutual support and fellowship, and one that sees the local church as 'the earthly heaven in which the heavenly God dwells and moves'.[12]

Given the remarks made earlier concerning the deadness that can so easily afflict congregational life, it may seem absurd to view the Church in such an elevated way. Plainly it is not 'without spot or blemish' as St Paul envisioned it. We can nevertheless continue to love it for, as Augustine discerned, the Church is made holy not by virtue of its membership but through the indwelling power of the Holy Spirit. This truth sustained him through long years of dealing with the moral and spiritual lapses of clergy and congregations—a point worth remembering when our own attempts at worship seem feeble and our human limitations are all too obvious. As long as we retain the capacity for renewal, and resolve to see God as somehow inextricably bound up with our offering of prayer and praise we can always be hopeful.

Notice though how in worship, as in the rest of life, so much hinges on the way we see. Our attention has been drawn to this on several occasions in previous chapters, and Jesus himself promised that the pure in heart would see God.[13] This proved a tantalizing and desirable prospect throughout Christian history, and many lives down the centuries pursued the vision at great cost. Monasticism and mysticism in their different ways offered adherents a road to God, provided they were single-minded and sincere in their pursuit. Without depicting the religious life as one of unremitting struggle is there not an important insight here? God discloses himself to the pure in heart—to those who think more clearly and feel more deeply—and who, as a consequence, acquire a depth that is not granted to everyone. There is nothing élitist about this; God has no favourites, and his rain falls on the just and the unjust alike.[14] But his truth, goodness, and beauty are not cheap commodities sold on the open market. They are given freely to those who pay honest attention to the particular and see beyond and beneath the surface of things.

Worship is no superficial performance; is not just a matter of words and symbols, of sounds and gestures. They each serve their purpose only insofar as they open our eyes to the reality of God expressed so directly in the opening words of the Te Deum: 'You are God and we praise you; you are the Lord and we acclaim you.' If we have become slow in our apprehension that worship is about the glory of the Lord, perhaps we have lost the sense that God is to be adored because he is the source of all beauty, and that his nature which has shone in the face of Jesus Christ is one which is supremely beautiful. Sadly, it has to be admitted that we have not always been encouraged to see worship as a vehicle for divine beauty. Following on from the Reformation, and in particular during the time of Cromwell's Commonwealth in the seventeenth century, so much innocent joy, song and dance, art and music came to be regarded as unspiritual and consequently fit only for suppression or destruction. Church organs were smashed, wall murals whitewashed, statues removed, buildings desecrated. Even now it is still said about many churches that: 'Cromwell stabled his horses here.'[15]

Mercifully, within the entire sweep of Christianity, this destructive attitude to beauty in all its forms can be seen as an aberration. The great gift of the Orthodox churches to Christianity lies in their power to perceive the beauty of the divine and express it in their worship, which is nothing less than 'heaven on earth'. An overwhelming sense of God's presence pervades their liturgy where not merely the local congregation are present but the entire Church—the communion of saints, angels and archangels, the Mother of God, and Christ himself. 'Now the celestial powers are present with us, and worship invisibly.'[16] In this knowledge, the Orthodox bring splendour and beauty to their worship; it has inspired their best poetry, art, and music, and is seen as an icon or intimation of the great Liturgy of heaven. On a more modest scale in nineteenth-century England the Oxford Movement[17] rediscovered the place of beauty in the religious life. Churches were adorned again; worship became a more resonant thing offering food for the eye and imagination as well as moral exhortation. The holiness and beauty of God were there to be discerned provided the eye of the mind was pure.

This would suggest that our longing for God and our capacity for adoration are crucially bound up with the sensitivity and honesty that we bring to the activity of worship. Purity of heart and mind are the essential prerequisites; they afford us a sensibility that discerns depths and dimensions which frequently go unacknowledged by those who simply cannot or will not pay attention. The beauty of form and face goes unperceived; the exquisite sound of voice and instrument fail to register; the fashioning of something beautiful evokes no response; and even the proclamation of the word of God in all its power and beauty leaves us untouched.

Yet the divine is in all these things; their beauty and therefore their truth is derived from the being of God himself. They invite our full attention, and to respond wholeheartedly is to be led beyond them to their source. What we see has to be related to what we think in our minds and judge in our hearts. If this sounds needlessly complicated we might just bear in mind that all artistic creation entails a struggle to express the truth. Why should it be any easier for us as we are challenged to apprehend it?

An inescapable conclusion confronts us here: something approaching a reasoned orderliness or a disciplined attitude is necessary if worship is to lead us to the vision of God as the goal of human life. Carelessness and indifference will always reap a lean harvest, and bad worship is often due to nothing more than a repeated unwillingness to bother. We miss the meaning and the glory because too little of ourselves has been involved in the activity.

In one sense this should not surprise us; worship is such a regular and predictable affair that it can easily become a fairly mundane routine. Repetition in all spheres of life is the enemy of passion, and spirituality like sensuality can become dulled by habit. The condition at its worst can lead to the sort of torpor that fails to respond creatively to the challenge of worship on the grounds that it is too much of an effort. More often than not though, when everything seems stale, we tend just to drift through services; words wash over us, faces pass us by, God seems a little remote. No one is free from this temptation, and it would be astonishing if a retrospective look at our church life did not indicate occasional troughs, perhaps even identifiable with particular periods of the year.

It pays to be on our guard then—to recognize the contours of the spiritual life and to be alert to early warning signs of lethargy. This holds true for all of us—clergy and congregation. Comparison with a marriage that is faltering because of boredom induced by familiarity and routine is not altogether inappropriate. If our worship is to be kept in good repair it needs regular scrutiny; not just in terms of language, hymns and ritual but at the deeper level where discipline and disposition have a huge bearing on the integrity of what we offer to God.

To read the religious instruction manuals of the Victorian age is to wonder that anyone could ever have fulfilled their requirements. Worshippers are advised to begin preparing for Communion days before: consciences are to be examined, passages studied, and sins called to mind. It is all very earnest and in keeping with the 'high mindedness' of our nineteenth-century forebears. Little place is given to levity or spontaneity, for worship is a solemn business. We can smile now at their pretensions and how they made the easy mistake of substituting solemnity for seriousness. We might also regret, however, the mistake that we make in the opposite direction—namely, the quite unwarranted presumptions that worship requires no form of preparation on our part, is not significantly affected by the attitudes we bring, and requires little from us by way of real participation. That, after all, is what we pay the clergy for; they 'make it happen'. I am exaggerating, but not overmuch. Worship will often seem threadbare because it lacks precious human resources: a spirit of expectation; a readiness to hear and understand what is being said; an awareness of the needs of others present; an appreciation of the cost that has already been incurred by way of preparation so that, potentially at least, our coming together might prove an enriching experience. It is within our power to do something about all these deficiencies but first we have to recognize them.

A more difficult matter concerns the ability and sensitivity of those who lead worship. Not infrequently the justifiable complaint is made that services are marred by the officiant or celebrant. They talk too much; they are overbearing and condescending; they have not held on to their brains and it shows in their preaching; they seem tired and induce tedium; they do not register our pain and we feel diminished as a consequence; they seem ill at ease with silence. At one level, all of these unfortunate traits can be described in terms of professional incompetence or pastoral insensitivity. What can be done in such situations will depend on the existing relationships between clergy, church officers, and congregation. If the truth can be spoken discreetly in love there is always the possibility of improvement—clergy are sometimes genuinely glad to be told that their leading of worship is problematic to others. If on the other hand an unspoken church protocol demands that the preceding issues are never acknowledged out of a desire to avoid confrontation or giving hurt, it is hard to see how services can be enhanced until the leadership changes.

Clergy carry a weighty responsibility for the conduct of worship, and it is proper that they should be accountable. But before judgement is passed or criticism lodged, how well do we understand the fact that they too are human and need help and encouragement like the rest of the congregation? I am reminded of a striking image in a book published some years ago;[18] a good deal of the content has now been forgotten but the picture remains. It is a Saturday night and in a vicarage a clergyman is crying in his wife's arms. He is in despair; he has two sermons to preach tomorrow and nothing, absolutely nothing to say. His mind is blank—no thoughts, no words. The readings give him no inspiration. Worst of all, he is acutely aware of his own emptiness and aloneness. The feeling comes too often but the sermons must be preached, the visits done, the roof repaired if it is falling in.

Those who have been ordained for more than a handful of years will recognize, to some extent at least, the feelings portrayed in the story. Clergy live with failure more often than is commonly realized; failure in themselves to embody fully the values proclaimed from the pulpit, and failure on the part of their congregations to be the Body of Christ. Preaching can easily become problematical as the years and disappointments increase. Clergy find themselves

> with little to say that they have not said before . . . doubtful of their own ability to expound and of their own right to exhort . . . and who detect, among those who have heard little remembrance of what they have said, and less effect. Such preachers . . . settle for the compromise of continuing to preach but at a lesser expenditure of care and time, and of doing badly that which they can see no adequate reason for doing at all.[19]

What should be done? The remedy is unlikely to be found in the latest book on the art of sermon construction. A recovery of nerve and vision is called for—a rekindling of the sense that preaching matters because it is an offering rendered in the service of God. It is a high calling—'a joyful tyranny'[20]—and though preachers may be conscious of their inadequacies or indifference to the task, surpassing both should be the knowledge that something of worth may be derived from the word that is spoken out of struggle and directed to the hearts and minds of those who will hear.

Congregations cannot shirk their responsibilities here. Great harm is done when the sermon comes to be regarded as a harmless interval in the proceedings when we can allow ourselves to be distracted by the slightest thing, entertain totally irrelevant thoughts, and generally appear uninterested to such an extent that the preacher quite properly over a period of time comes to think that energy given to preaching might better be spent on the crossword. We have no right to trifle with the word of God. It will only become 'living and active'[21] and take a hold on our lives when we actually engage with the sermon, and align ourselves with the preacher so that together we might learn from and be changed by the offering. There is a subtle dialectic to be observed in preaching. Clergy do not preach out of their own strength alone or simply by the grace of God. They derive their energy in part from their relationship with those in front of them, who by their obvious attention, or palpable lack of it, have the power to make the sermon a creative event or a stillborn utterance.

Priest and people need each other. I am mindful again of Augustine, this time preaching to his congregations all those centuries ago in an age as uncertain as our own. He would speak to the faithful from his bishop's chair, not from some remote pulpit. The people would stand just a yard or so away from him, and his words often moved them to tears. Augustine himself would be visibly affected by the occasion, and no one present could be in any doubt that something of significance was taking place. The same kind of symbiosis can be seen in the recordings we still possess of Martin Luther King rallying his people to the cause of racial justice in the turbulent America of the 1960s. What we witness there is not simply incandescent oratory but a marvellously creative exchange whereby the energy and will of the listeners are harnessed in such a way that they become part of the proclamation.

An important lesson can be drawn from these two examples, and it has to do with the fact that preaching is actually a form of pastoral care that has the power to bind a congregation together.[22] This may well seem a strange notion to anyone who has grown weary over the years with the sort of preaching that never gets beyond exhortation and recrimination. This usually has the dismal effect of compounding feelings of unworthiness and inadequacy on the part of those who can bear to heed the sermon, and casts the preacher in the role of martinet—an essentially authoritarian figure and quite unapproachable. But it does not have to be this way. As preachers we are free to leave the pulpit on occasions and come down to our people. To be on their level may help us to recognize them as travellers on the same road and not miscreants in need of correction. And if we have something to say, its importance and immediacy may touch those present in a new way simply because they feel involved with us—can see us, can sense that we are being exercised by the message and its relevance for our lives as well as theirs.

A little humanity on the part of the preacher goes a long way in worship, and reinforces the point made earlier that clergy and congregations need each other. Priest and people are interdependent. The work of worship is a shared venture; our personalities and the quality of our relationships are the vehicles through which God works. Leaving aside the relationship between the congregation and those set over it as servants, we need to say something now about the congregation itself and the rapport worshippers share with each other.

Most of us need the support of companions and community if we are to grow in the ways of holiness. This is a sign of health not weakness, for it acknowledges that we are learners, able to receive wisdom and correction from others. The congregation is where we learn to worship, and come to love God more. The great Spanish mystic Teresa of Avila reminds us that: 'If you would know God you must frequent the company of his friends.' In this respect the image of those who assemble together Sunday by Sunday is both striking and flattering; we are presented with the people of God, convened to sing his praise and to share in the love, joy, and peace of the gospel. We receive the assurance of sins forgiven and our strength is renewed for our work in the world. The reality of course is often quite different. It is just as easy to be alone in a congregation as it is to be alone in a crowd. It is perfectly possible for a network of relationships to exist in a worshipping community which are so superficial that the Eucharist itself becomes little more than a celebration of alienation. One of the more radical truths of Christianity still to be appropriated by the Church is that we do not choose our brothers and sisters in Christ—they are given to us. We are indebted to, and, paradoxically, responsible for the person beside, behind, and in front of us. We may not know them, and if we do, may not particularly care for them; and yet our shared status as members of a community under God welds us inextricably together. If we can put it this way, the horizontal aspect of worship matters as much as the vertical. Relationships have to be worked at, fostered, and nurtured; cliques and rampant individualism alike vitiate worship.

St Paul is clearly unhappy with the community at Corinth when he writes: 'Your meetings tend to do more harm than good . . . when you meet as a congregation you fall into sharply divided groups.'[23] This is to make nonsense of Paul's teaching on the Church as the Body of Christ[24] and the importance of its shared life. In the early Christian church the word '*koinonia*' was used to illuminate this truth. '*Koinonia*' is a Greek word meaning both 'communion' and 'community' and the former is a prerequisite of the latter. To break bread together (which is of course a significant act in every Eucharist) is to acknowledge that those who worship with us are companions not strangers. The word 'companions' comes from the Latin '*con*' meaning 'with' and '*panis*' meaning 'bread'. Companions are the people with whom we share bread, and each celebration of the Eucharist therefore is a communal event fostering a proper sense of dependence on others.

We might also call to mind that the Christian understanding of God from the earliest centuries has been expressed in terms of Father and Son in the fellowship of the Holy Spirit. We hear this formula so often that it is easy to overlook what is being asserted—nothing less than the 'social character' of God. We cannot stray into the notoriously complex field of trinitarian theology but the essential point is, I think, made by Professor J. M. Lochman when he comments 'God means community because he is community in his essence.'[25] These insights should caution us if we are ever tempted to make worship a purely private affair; taken to heart and lived out more evidently they have the power to transform our church life.[25].

During this chapter we have considered some of the reasons why worship is sometimes a sorry experience, and what might be done to address the underlying problems. I want to close by emphasizing the importance in worship of what I can only describe as moral passion. This may seem a peculiar turn of phrase, so a word of explanation. We are so used to understanding worship in terms of ritual—as a particular and repetitive way of doing things (whether a High Mass or a simple service of hymns and readings)—that its worth and value tend to be judged largely in terms of performance. We often say the choir sang beautifully, the sermon was well crafted, the readings and prayers were intelligibly rendered, and the congregation participated well. Note how in each case the emphasis is placed on expertise or competence. Quite rightly we might add, for we should give only our best—'hearts and minds and hands and voices in our choicest psalmody'.[26] But underpinning everything that is offered there should be moral passion— a longing for the reign of peace and love; an awareness of the world's tragic wonder; a humbling knowledge of our own ragged humanity; and a firm hope that all our tomorrows are held in the providence of God. To bring this kind of sensibility to worship is to invest it with a dignity, depth, and authenticity which transform a competent performance into an offering of genuine worth.

Moral passion is a consequence of learning to see aright— learning, that is, to love the world passionately in all its grief and grandeur without illusions. When we pray together with the Psalmist that: 'The needy shall not always be forgotten nor shall the hope of the poor perish for ever',[27] we are not just reciting a poignant verse from Scripture; we are effectively committing ourselves to the struggle for life and liberty on behalf of the poor and needy. And when we have done the best we can, only to realize that wickedness and oppression continue unabated, we do not lose heart because we know that we have done (and must continue to do) the right thing—we have been faithful to the truth that our moral vision has disclosed to us. More than this, we learn to be patient for we have come to see ourselves as we truly are (that is, wonderfully made but with a talent for waywardness), and we have accepted that the fulfilment of our hopes may lie beyond the wrecks of time in 'an age to come' when history with all its hurts and sorrows is transformed into the realm of the eternal. And always—in worship as in life—we look to God for 'all times are his seasons.'[28]

> Too soon we rise, the symbols disappear
> The feast, though not the love is past and gone
> The bread and wine remove but thou art here
> Nearer than ever, still our shield and sun.[29]

FOR REFLECTION

Cups

Can you drink of this cup?
The cup I drink.
Cup of sorrow.
Can you bear betrayal, desertion, despair?
Can you drink of this cup,
Cup of sin.
Can you see your own face,
Reflected in the wine?
Can you see your own life,
Caught in the cup?
Cup of sacrifice.

Can you drink of this cup?
The cup I drink.
Cup of solace.
Can you share compassion, companionship, hope?
Can you drink of this cup,
Cup of acceptance.
Can you see your own face,
Reflected in the wine?
Can you see your own life,
Caught in the cup?
Cup of rejoicing.

(Ann Youle)

THE BIG QUESTIONS

A Meditation on the Indwelling Christ

In the beginning was the Word; and the Word was with God; and the Word was God.

And the Word was made flesh.

In You, Jesus, the Eternal Word, which was with the Father from the beginning, became incarnate in time and history. You were born; You spoke of truth; You were crucified; You rose again; You ascended into the Radiance of the Eternal.

And now I know that in ascending You at the same time descended. You are still here, still dwelling on this earth, always and everywhere present, living in my heart. Now all hearts which open to You have become Your Bethlehem, Your Galilee, Your Calvary, Your Resurrection garden.

> Thou who livest within my heart,
> Awaken me to the immensity of Thy spirit,
> To the experience of Thy living presence!
> Deliver me from the bonds of desire,
> From the slavery of small aims,
> From the delusion of narrow egohood!

> Enlighten me with the light of Thy wisdom,
> Suffuse me with the radiance of Thy love,
> Which includes and embraces the darkness,
> Like the light which surrounds the dark core of the flame,
> Like the love of a mother that surrounds
> The growing life in the darkness of the womb,
> Like the earth protecting the tender germ of the seed.

Lord, come to us that Thou mayest cleanse us; Lord, come to us that Thou mayest heal us; Lord, come to us that Thou mayest strengthen us; and grant that, having received Thee, we may never be separated from Thee, but may continue Thine for ever and ever; for Jesus Christ's sake.

Let all mortal flesh keep silence, and with fear and trem-
bling stand;
Ponder nothing earthly-minded, for with blessing in His
hand,
Christ our God to earth descendeth, our full homage to
demand.

King of Kings, yet born of Mary, as of old on earth He stood,
Lord of Lords, in human vesture—in the Body and the
Blood—
He will give to all the faithful His own Self for heavenly
food.

Rank on rank the host of heaven spreads its vanguard on the
way,
As the Light of light descendeth from the realms of endless
day,
That the powers of hell may vanish as the darkness clears
away.

At His feet the six-winged Seraph: Cherubim with sleepless
eye,
Veil their faces to the Presence, as with ceaseless voice they
cry,
Alleluya, Alleluya, Alleluya, Lord most high.

O salutaris hostia

O saving victim! opening wide
The gates of heaven to man below.
Our foes press hard on every side—
Thine aid supply, Thy strength bestow.

All praise and thanks to Thee ascend
For evermore, blest One in Three;
O grant us life which shall not end
In our true native land with Thee.

THE BIG QUESTIONS

Tantum ergo

Therefore we, before Thee bending,
This great Sacrament revere;
Types and shadows have their ending
But the newer rite is here;
Faith, our outward sense befriending,
Makes the inward vision clear.

Glory let us give and blessing
To the Father and the Son;
Honour, might and praise addressing,
While eternal ages run;
Ever too His love confessing,
Who, from both, with both is one.

A Collect for Sundays

O God, you make us glad with the weekly remembrance of the glorious resurrection of your Son our Lord: Give us this day such blessing through our worship of you, that the week to come may be spent in your favor; through Jesus Christ our Lord. Amen.

A Collect for Fridays

Almighty God, whose most dear Son went not up to joy but first he suffered pain, and entered not into glory before he was crucified: Mercifully grant that we, walking in the way of the cross, many find it none other than the way of life and peace; through Jesus Christ your Son our Lord. Amen.

ALL TIMES ARE HIS SEASONS
A Collect for Saturdays

Almighty God, who after the creation of the world rested from all your works and sanctified a day of rest for all your creatures: Grant that we, putting away all earthly anxieties, may be duly prepared for the service of your sanctuary, and that our rest here upon earth may be a preparation for the eternal rest promised to your people in heaven; through Jesus Christ our Lord. Amen.

A Collect for the Renewal of Life

O God, the King eternal, whose light divides the day from the night and turns the shadow of death into the morning: Drive far from us all wrong desires, incline our hearts to keep your law, and guide our feet into the way of peace; that, having done your will with cheerfulness during the day, we may, when night comes, rejoice to give you thanks; through Jesus Christ our Lord. Amen.

A Collect for Peace

O God, the author of peace and lover of concord, to know you is eternal life and to serve you is perfect freedom: Defend us, your humble servants, in all assaults of our enemies; that we, surely trusting in your defence, may not fear the power of any adversaries; through the might of Jesus Christ our Lord. Amen.

Strengthen for service, Lord, the hands that have taken holy things; may the ears which have heard your word be deaf to clamour and dispute; may the tongues which have sung your praise be free from deceit; may the eyes which have seen the tokens of your love shine with the light of hope; and may the bodies which have been fed with your body be refreshed with the fulness of your life; glory to you for ever.

(Liturgy of Malabar)

NOTES

*

CHAPTER 1

1. This incident is recounted by Peter Berger in his book *A Rumour of Angels* (Pelican, 1973), Ch. 5.
2. See *Unfinished Agenda*, Ch. 18; Lesslie Newbigin's autobiography (SPCK, 1985).
3. The lectures are now available in paperback under the title *The Persistence of Faith* by Jonathan Sacks (Weidenfeld, 1991).
4. Judges 21.25.
5. See Genesis 9.1–17 for the scriptural account of the covenant. G. Von Rad provides helpful insights into the passage in his masterful commentary on Genesis: see Ch. 2, section 12 (SCM, 1976).
6. Based on the passage from Genesis 2.23.
7. Cited in Owen Chadwick, *The Secularisation of the European Mind in the Nineteenth Century* (CUP, 1975).
8. *Honest to God* was first published in 1963 by SCM, and subsequently went through many impressions. Outside of the Bible, it is probably the most widely read religious book of the twentieth century.
9. The series was entitled 'Priestland's Progress'.
10. John 3.16.
11. See John 1.1–14; and 1 John 1.
12. Taken from John Betjeman's poem 'Christmas' in *The Best of Betjeman* (Penguin, 1978).
13. Exodus 3.13–14.
14. Romans 11.33–34.
15. Richard Dawkins is the most prominent (and controversial) exponent of this view; see his *The Selfish Gene* (OUP, 1976).
16. Jeremiah 33.22.
17. Acts 17.28.
18. Jeremiah 10.12–16 is a good example of the Hebraic concept of God.
19. Psalm 100.2.
20. From the Prayer of General Confession in the Book of Common Prayer (1662).
21. Genesis 5.1.
22. Martin Buber, *I and Thou* (T. & T. Clark, 1959), p. 135.

NOTES

23. ARCIC (Anglican-Roman Catholic International Commission), *The Final Report* (CTS/SPCK, 1982), pp. 69–70.
24. Romans 1.3–4; Galatians 1.1.
25. John 14.6.

CHAPTER 2

1. Gregory Dix, *The Shape of the Liturgy* (A. & C. Black, 1978), p. 745.
2. F. C. Happold, *Prayer and Meditation* (Pelican, 1971), p. 105,.
3. Matthew 5.48.
4. Brian Keenan, *An Evil Cradling* (Vintage, 1993), p. 99.
5. Deuteronomy 6.5.
6. For examples, see Mark 1.12–13, 35; 14.32–36.
7. For an interesting discussion of this point, see J. H. Newman *On Consulting the Faithful in Matters of Doctrine* (Collins Flame Classics, 1986), pp. 75–6. Newman is concerned to show that during the doctrinal controversies of the early centuries (post-Nicean Council AD 325) it was ordinary believers who were the strength of the Church. At a time when bishops failed in their confession of the faith and spoke against each other, the body of the laity was faithful to its baptism. Under Providence they maintained the Church in truth.
8. From J. Ellerton's hymn 'The day thou gavest Lord is ended', in *Hymns Ancient and Modern Revised* (The Canterbury Press, 1875).
9. From the prelude to the Sanctus in the Communion Service.
10. A good contemporary example is Sister Wendy Beckett, now known to millions of viewers following her television series on famous paintings. She lives in a caravan without radio or television and spends seven hours each day in prayer.
11. Mark 4.3–9.
12. 1 Corinthians 6.19.
13. From 'The Circus Animals' Desertion' by W. B. Yeats in the *New Oxford Book of English Verse* (Oxford, 1972).
14. Mark 7.20–23.
15. 1 Peter 4.7.
16. E. de Waal, *A Seven Day Journey with Thomas Merton* (Eagle, 1992), p. 29.
17. John 10.10.
18. Romans 8.21.
19. From 'Auguries of Innocence' by William Blake in *William Blake* (Penguin, 1970).
20. Romans 7.24.
21. 2 Corinthians 11.28.
22. Philippians 3.8.
23. Ephesians 4.13.

NOTES

24. Joseph Butler (1692–1752), Bishop of Durham and among the greatest exponents of natural theology and ethics in England since the Reformation.
25. From T. S. Eliot, 'Four Quartets', *East Coker* Part 5 in *The Complete Poems and Plays* (Faber & Faber, 1969).
26. Michael Ramsey, Archbishop of Canterbury 1961–1974.
27. Charles Peguy refers to the Christian as 'the burden bearer of creation', quoted by Alan Ecclestone in *Yes to God* (DLT, 1975).
28. T. S. Eliot, *Murder in the Cathedral*, Part 1, second chorus, in *The Complete Poems and Plays* (Faber & Faber, 1969).
29. Ephesians 4.17–19.
30. Deuteronomy 30.19.
31. Quoted by M. Furlong in *Travelling In* (Hodder & Stoughton, 1971), p. 53.
32. This is an important principle in theology, intended to show that divine grace does not replace human nature but perfects it (originally attributed to Thomas Aquinas).
33. From C. Wesley's hymn, 'O thou who camest from above', *Hymn 329* in *Hymns Ancient and Modern Revised* (Canterbury Press, 1875).

CHAPTER 3

1. Examples would include Psalms 16, 22, 73, 88, and 116.
2. Job 42.1–6.
3. Ecclesiastes 3.7.
4. Job 2.13.
5. Leviticus 10.3.
6. Romans 9.19–21.
7. Mark 15.33–34.
8. For examples, see Dan Cohn-Sherbok, *Holocaust Theology* (Lamp Press, 1989).
9. Genesis 18.25.
10. John Hick, *Evil and the God of Love* (Collins, 1968), p. 360.
11. Questions originally posed by H. J. McCloskey, 'God and Evil', *Philosophical Quarterly*, 10 (1960), pp. 97–114.
12. The clockmaker model of God popularized in the eighteenth century: '. . . the manifold appearance of design and final causes in the construction of the world prove it to be the work of an intelligent mind . . .' Joseph Butler (1692–1752), philosopher and cleric. This quotation is from his *Analogy of Religion Natural and Revealed* (1736), Ch. 3.
13. John Polkinghorne, *Science and Providence* (SPCK, 1989), Ch. 5, p. 67.
14. Romans 8.22.
15. William Vanstone, *Love's Endeavour Love's Expense* (DLT, 1977), Ch. 4, p. 63.
16. Vanstone, *Love's Endeavour*, p. 62.

17. William Shakespeare, *Sonnets*, 116.
18. Philippians 2.7–9.
19. Colossians 1.15.
20. Jürgen Moltmann, *The Crucified God* (SCM, 1972), p. 205.
21. For a helpful treatment of this subject, see Hans Küng, *The Incarnation of God* (T. & T. Clark, 1987), pp. 518–25.
22. Timothy Rees, 'God is Love', from *100 Hymns for Today* (W. Clowes & Sons, 1969).
23. Mark 15.39.
24. John 19.30.
25. These insights are derived from a helpful essay by David Brown, 'The Problem of Pain' in *The Religion of the Incarnation* (Bristol Classic Press, 1989).
26. Revelation 21.4.
27. Stendhal: pseudonym of Mari Heni Beyle (1783–1842); source of quote unknown.

CHAPTER 4

1. Francis Kilvert, *Journal of a Country Curate* (Folio Society, 1977), p. 327.
2. First line of J. Addison's famous hymn, *Hymn 170* in *Hymns Ancient and Modern Revised* (The Canterbury Press, 1875).
3. Bertrand Russell, English philosopher (1872–1970). See his autobiography (Allen & Unwin, Vol. 1 1967, Vol. 2 1968) for a full treatment of his views.
4. Quoted from p. 9 of J. Bowker's *The Meanings of Death* (Cambridge, 1991).
5. Sigmund Freud (1856–1939), Austrian founder of psychoanalysis; see his *The Future of an Illusion* (Hogarth Press, 1928) for his controversial view of religion.
6. Freud, *The Future*, p. 14.
7. Freud saw the same twelve patients every day, six days a week (and then wrote late into the night). This, to say the least, provides meagre data on which to base theories that presume universal application.
8.   Indeed if we permit ourselves the same speculations about him that he . . . has permitted himself about Moses and Leonardo da Vinci we may wonder whether his own unresolved conflict and intensely charged feelings about his father were not, perhaps as much responsible for his views about conscience and religion . . . as were any of his scientific abilities.

   This is a quotation from D. Stafford Clark, *Five Questions in Search of an Answer* (Fontana, 1970), p. 18.
9. 1 Corinthians 2.9 (see also Isaiah 64.4).
10. Quoted from H. A. Williams' *True Resurrection* (Mitchell Beazley, 1972), p. 178.

NOTES

11. Ephesians 3.20.
12. Revelation 21.18–19.
13.   . . . death,
      The undiscover'd country from whose bourn
      No traveller returns . . .
    from the famous soliloquy in Shakespeare's *Hamlet*, Act 3, Scene 1.
14. 1 Peter 3.21–2.
15. See H. J. Cadbury, 'Intimations of Immortality in the Thought of Jesus', in Krister Stendhal (ed.), *Immortality and Resurrection* (Macmillan, New York, 1965), p. 139–140.
16. From *Through the Looking Glass* (Penguin, 1984) by Lewis Carroll (1832–1898).
17. 'Religionless Christianity' is linked to the writings of Dietrich Bonhoeffer, who died at the hands of the SS aged 39. In a passage from a famous letter of 30 April, 1944 he writes:

    I am constantly moved by the question of what Christianity really is, or who Christ really is for us today. The time in which everything could be said to men by means of words, whether theological or pious, is over. So too is the time of inwardness or conscience, which means the time of religion in general. We are moving towards a completely religionless time. Men as they are simply cannot be religious any more.

    For a concise and helpful appraisal of Bonhoeffer's thought, see W. Nicholls' *Penguin Guide to Modern Theology* (Penguin, 1969), Vol. 1, pp. 192–232 and D. F. Ford (ed.) *The Modern Theologians* (Blackwell, 1989), pp. 50–69.
18. For an introduction to liberation theology, especially in its Latin American context, see Ford, *Modern Theologians*, Ch. 9.
19. 'Christ being raised from the dead dieth no more; death hath no dominion over him.' (Romans 6.9).
20. 1 Corinthians 13.12.
21. From F. W. Faber's hymn 'My God, how wonderful thou art', in *Hymns Ancient and Modern Revised* (The Canterbury Press, 1875).
22. H. H. Price, *Essays in the Philosophy of Religion* (OUP, 1972), p. 84.
23. Words attributed to Mother Julian of Norwich, English mystic (1342–after 1413).
24. From John Donne, quoted in *By Heart: A Lifetime Companion* by John Bowden (ed.) (SCM, 1985), p. 50. Donne was a poet and Dean of St Paul's (1571/2–1631).
25. We can take encouragement from those members of the communion of Saints who have put their imagination to work in the service of their fellow Christians. St. Augustine, Julian of Norwich, Dante, Thomas Traherne, C. S. Lewis, Austin Farrer . . . these are some who have thought it right and fitting to hearten us with positive images of God's purposes.

NOTES

This is taken from H. Oppenheimer, *Looking Before and After* (Collins Fount, 1988), p. 131.

26. Final lines of 'Once in royal David's city', in *Hymns Ancient and Modern Revised* (The Canterbury Press, 1875).
27. Psalm 46.10.
28. From the autobiography of J. S. Mill (OUP World's Classics), p. 112.
29. From T. S. Eliot, 'Ash Wednesday 1930' Section 6, in the *Complete Poems and Plays* (Faber & Faber, 1969).
30. Alternative Service Book 1980, p. 104.
31. As one of many examples, see Colossians 1.15–20.
32. John 3.16 and 1 John 4.9.
33. From the Anglican funeral service, ASB, p. 316.
34. See 1 Corinthians 15.35–58. Note also that the Apostles' Creed and the Nicene Creed make no reference to a belief in the immortality of the soul.
35. 1 Corinthians 15.22.
36. 1 Peter 1.3–4.
37. For a proper treatment of these questions, see J. Hick, *Death and Eternal Life* (Collins, 1976), Ch. 15.
38. Cited by Oppenheimer, *Looking Before*, p. 131.
39. Attributed to the writer and poet, George Meredith (1828–1909).
40. Quotation provided by Reverend C. P. Burkett, source unknown.
41. Romans 8.31, 35–8.

CHAPTER 5

1. Martin Buber, *Hasidim and Modern Man* (Harper & Row, 1966), p. 159, (adapted).
2. Matthew 25.14–30.
3. Alexander Pope, *An Essay on Man*, Epistle 2.
4. From 'Dust', *The Collected Poems of Elizabeth Jennings* (Carcanet, 1987), p. 212.
5. St Irenaeus (*c.* 130–200), Bishop of Lyons.
6. The era of the Fathers began some time in the first century and concluded in the East around the year 750. They were a defined group of ecclesiastical writers whose authority on doctrinal matters carried special weight.
7. Several Greek fathers identify 'the likeness of God' with free will or in a quality of the human soul such as immortality or reason. The scriptural reference is Genesis 1.26.
8. 2 Peter 1.4.
9. 2 Corinthians 3.18.
10. This is how C. K. Barrett describes St Paul's doctrine of human nature in the Epistle to the Romans. See Barrett's excellent commentary on the epistle in *Epistle to the Romans* (A. & C. Black, 1991).

NOTES

11. Attributed to Blaise Pascal, French philosopher and theologian (1623–1662).

12. See Martin Luther's famous hymn 'A safe stronghold our God is still', in *Hymns Ancient and Modern Revised* (The Canterbury Press, 1875).

13. Professor Gunther Bornkamm; cited by Antony Bridge in *One Man's Advent* (Fount, 1986), p. 117.

14. Matthew 7.24–7.

15. Source unknown, translation by Samuel Beckett.

16. Isaiah 53.3.

17. George Eliot, *The Mill on the Floss* (Pan, 1973), pp. 271, 284.

18. Psalm 139.13.

19. Luke 4.16.

20. A point that frequently goes unnoticed is that Jesus did belong to a large family with brothers and sisters; see Mark 6.3.

21. From Thomas à Kempis, *The Imitation of Christ* (Methuen, 1921).

22. For a full and fascinating treatment of this subject see P. Brown, *The Body and Society*, (Faber & Faber, 1989).

23. See in particular Brown, 'The Early Middle Ages' in *The Body and Society*, pp. 428ff.

24. Brown, *The Body and Society*, p. 442.

25. From Augustine's work, *Seeing God the Inexpressible*, p. 102.

26. Acts 2.42–5.

27. From the Introduction to the Marriage Service, ASB.

28. 1 Corinthians 13.5–7.

29. Bishop Joseph Butler (1692–1752). *Analogy of Religion* was written to inquirers unconvinced of the claims of religion. The book is remarkable for the closely knit texture of its argument.

30. Ephesians 2.10.

31. A. Ridler (ed.), *Thomas Traherne. Poems, Centuries and Three Thanksgivings* (London, 1966), p. 177.

32. Song of Solomon 8.7.

33. Dylan Thomas, *Miscellany One* (J. M. Dent, 1972), p. 26.

34. Story taken from A. M. Allchin, *The World Is a Wedding* (DLT, 1978), p. 24.

35. Based on John 1.5.

36. Primo Levi's book, *Other People's Trades* (Michael Joseph, 1989), is a marvellous example of how deep significance is to be found in the apparently ordinary and unremarkable.

37. From the poems of William Blake, quoted by J. Bronowski in *William Blake and the Age of Revolution* (Routledge and Kegan Paul, 1972), p. 182.

NOTES

CHAPTER 6

1. Revelation 3.15–17.
2. See my article 'The Thought of St. Augustine', *Churchman*, Vol. 104, No. 4, p. 346.
3. Isaiah 29.13.
4. For an interesting account of eighteenth-century Anglican religion, see R. Porter *English Society in the Eighteenth Century* (Pelican, 1982), pp. 184–92.
5. This striking term is used by K. E. Kirk in his classic work *The Vision of God* (J. Clarke & Co., reissue 1991). See page 46 (phrase originally attributed to M. Bremond).
6. See Luke 15.11–24 and closing prayer of thanksgiving in the ASB Communion Service.
7. Isaiah 6.1–3.
8. Genesis 28.10–13.
9. From George Herbert's poem 'Prayer' in *A Choice of George Herbert's Verse* (Faber & Faber, 1967).
10. The seminal work on this subject is R. Otto, *The Idea of the Holy* (OUP, 1924).
11. 1 Kings 19.11–13.
12. Quote attributed to Germanus, Patriarch of Constantinople (died 733).
13. Matthew 5.8.
14. Matthew 5.35.
15. See D. L. Edwards, *Christian England* (Fount, 1984), Vol. 2, pp. 289–99.
16. These words are sung at the Great Entrance in the Liturgy of the Presanctified.
17. For an account of the Oxford Movement, see S. Neill, *Anglicanism* (Mowbrays, 1977), pp. 254–61.
18. J. Bowden, *Voices in the Wilderness* (SCM, 1977).
19. Vanstone, *Love's Endeavour*, p. 111.
20. Donald Coggan, former Archbishop of Canterbury, liked to describe preaching as 'a joyful tyranny'.
21. Hebrews 4.12.
22.   Pastoral care must then be, in the last analysis, care for God's people, yet we must agree that the best fulfilment of the task occurs when the one to whom the flock are entrusted and the flock themselves are at one before God, united with the central act of Christ's pastoral care in the worship of the Church.

    This is taken from an essay by Joseph Pascher published in Germany in a volume entitled *Aus der Theologie der Zeit* (ed. G. Sotingen), (Regensburg, 1948).
23. 1 Corinthians 11.17–18.
24. 1 Corinthians 12.14–26.

NOTES

25. Jan Milic Lochman, 'The Trinity and Human Life', *Theology* (April 1975), p. 179.
26. From the hymn 'Angel voices ever singing' in *Hymns Ancient and Modern Revised* (The Canterbury Press, 1875).
27. Psalm 9.18.
28. John Donne in LXXX Sermons 1640 (preached at St Paul's upon Christmas Day 1624). Cited by A. R. Peacocke, *Creation and the World of Science* (Oxford, 1979), p. 359.
29. From the hymn 'Here, O my Lord I see thee Face to Face', No. 608, Vol. 4, *Hymns and Psalms* (Methodist Publishing House, 1983).